A GUIDE TO NEW JERSEY'S
REVOLUTIONARY WAR TRAIL

A GUIDE TO NEW JERSEY'S

REVOLUTIONARY WAR TRAIL

FOR FAMILIES AND HISTORY BUFFS

Mark Di Ionno

RUTGERS UNIVERSITY PRESS

NEW BRUNSWICK, NEW JERSEY,
AND LONDON

Fourth paperback printing, 2006

This book has been made possible in part by a gift from the Board of Governors of Rutgers, The State University of New Jersey, in honor of Anne Moreau Thomas for her many years of service, including three terms as Chair of the Board of Governors, during which she has brought her indispensable assets of strong leadership, calm judgment and love of Rutgers to the betterment of all members of our University community.

LIBRARY OF CONGRESS CATALOGING-IN-PUBLICATION DATA

Di Ionno, Mark.
    A guide to New Jersey's Revolutionary War trail for families and history buffs / Mark Di Ionno.
        p.   cm.
    Includes bibliographical references and index.
    ISBN 0-8135-2769-4 (cloth : alk. paper).   —   ISBN 0-8135-2770-8 (pbk. : alk. paper).
    1. New Jersey—History—Revolution, 1775–1783.   2. New Jersey—History—
Revolution, 1775–1783—Battlefields Guidebooks.   3. New Jersey—History—Revolution,
1775–1783—Monuments Guidebooks.   4. Historic sites—New Jersey Guidebooks.
5. United States—History—Revolution, 1775–1783—Battlefields Guidebooks.
6. United States—History—Revolution, 1775–1783—Monuments Guidebooks.
I. Title.
E263.N5D5   2000
974.9'03—dc21
                                                                99-43167
                                                                CIP

British Cataloging-in-Publication data for this book is available from the British Library

For my parents, Anthony Di Ionno and Rose (Tricarico) Di Ionno,
who taught their children to work hard, and to get out and learn

CONTENTS

ILLUSTRATIONS

ACKNOWLEDGMENTS

The first and biggest thanks go to my wife, Sharon. Without her support, this book would have been impossible. She allowed me to take significant time away from our family to first research, then write, this book—all in the face of the relentless challenge of raising four children under the age of six.

I'd also like to thank all the people from the county and community historical societies for their help. Many are mentioned in the pages that follow.

In my travels around the state, I often had a number of "research assistants" in tow to give me a good barometer of how interesting a site was for kids. These assistants include Anthony, Michelle, Stephanie, Matthew, Mark Jr., Laura, Christopher, and Mike Di Ionno; Jeffrey, Allison, and Colin Mechanic; Brittany and Allysa Homer; Kevin Finlay and Robby, Nicky, Katie, and Timmy Kaiser.

Thanks to my proofreaders, Dee Segal and Giovanna Fabiano, and to computer wizard Irv Bank, who got my manuscript user-friendly.

A GUIDE TO NEW JERSEY'S REVOLUTIONARY WAR TRAIL

Introduction

I am not a historian, and this is not a book about history. This is a book about discovery.

I remember very clearly the first time I discovered something about New Jersey history. It was in a Newberry's dime store in a strip mall in downtown Springfield. I was six or seven at the time.

The strip mall was across the street from the Presbyterian Church, where a Minuteman statue stands proud, commemorating the Battle of Springfield.

That battle was a fairly fierce campaign in which some seventy-five hundred Continental army regulars and New Jersey militiamen repelled a British force of six thousand.

I would learn about the particulars much later. But on this day, what I saw on a wall at Newberry's was a color mural depicting the action—a mural that appealed to a little boy's imagination.

The mural had a line of soldiers getting ready to fire at oncoming British troops. In the foreground was a man, not dressed like a soldier, shouting instructions. Along the bottom of the mural were the words, "Now give 'em Watts, boys!"

I asked my father what the mural was all about. He told me some of the story. His abbreviated version was about the Fighting Parson, the Reverend James Caldwell. A parson, my dad told me, was a like a priest, and although Caldwell was a man of God, he believed in the colonial fight for freedom, even if it meant killing enemy soldiers. "Watts" referred to the church hymnals, which contained the works of the famous hymn-writer Isaac

The Minuteman, Battle of Springfield Monument

Watts. Caldwell tore the hymnals up so the American soldiers could pack their muskets with the paper. "Now give 'em Watts, boys!" was a veiled way of saying, "Now shoot 'em!"

My father also told me that the very spot where we were standing—in the middle of Newberry's—had been part of the battlefield. And down the street was a house that had been hit by a cannonball, and you could still see the dent in it.

He told me that George Washington had been in the area, had probably ridden right up the street.

I knew, of course, who George Washington was, but he seemed very distant from me, not only in time but in geography. All the important things in American history, I learned in school, happened somewhere else—New England, Virginia, New York, Philadelphia.

But now I knew something else was true: George Washington fought battles near our house. I remember thinking that I lived somewhere special . . . a place that was important to America . . . a place you could be proud of.

You can imagine my disappointment, then, when I learned about the American Revolution in school. In school, the Revolution happened somewhere else. We learned all about Lexington and Yorktown, and not much about Trenton and Monmouth. We learned about the hard winter at Valley Forge, and nothing about Jockey Hollow.

We heard the legendary quotes: William Prescott's "Don't fire 'til you see the whites of their eyes" at Bunker Hill and John Paul Jones's "I have not yet begun to fight" aboard the *Bonhomme Richard*. We never heard the Fighting Parson's "Now give 'em Watts, boys!"

Perhaps that's why my interest in New Jersey history went dormant for nearly three decades. My reinforcements never came.

I became interested in New Jersey history not through education, but by accident.

I was born and raised in New Jersey. When I went away and joined the navy to see the world, they put me in Philadelphia. For much of the time I served there, I lived in South Jersey. After the service, I went to college, first at Rutgers College, New Brunswick, then at Rutgers-Newark. I've worked at three newspapers in the state and I've lived in fifteen Jersey towns in six Jersey counties.

For most of that time, I was only mildly curious about the state.

For the early part of my newspaper career I was a sportswriter. In 1985 I began working for the *New York Post* and soon became a columnist. During this time, when I had a job most people envied, I began to consider what I truly wanted to write about. The games and seasons began to blend into one, and I got tired of spending my creative energy on athletes. As a New York journalist I also got tired of hearing my home state denigrated as either a network of boring bedroom communities where artistic spirit is dulled by suburban sameness, or a chemical-industrial wasteland filled with gritty blue-collar drones living week to week, beer to beer. I got tired of all those stupid Turnpike jokes.

I left the *Post* in October 1990 and began writing for *The Star-Ledger.* In the search for feature stories, I began exploring my home state. I spent as much time on the road as I could, traveling the state, meeting its people and doing the best I could to tell their stories. I drove the rocky hills of the Highlands, got lost in the Pinelands, marveled at the desolation of the lower Delaware Bay. I discovered the rural beauty of the Upper Delaware Valley, where the Protestant steeples jut out over the rolling hills like sailboat masts on the high seas. I discovered the different Jersey Shores: the Victorian hamlets of Ocean Grove, Spring Lake, and Cape May; the honky-tonk of Keansburg, Seaside, and Wildwood; the cedar-shingled elegance of Bay Head and the Levittown-by-the-sea sprawl of Ocean Beach just a few miles down the road. I found the weird and the wonderful: the Dover psychologist who built totem poles; the car parts magnate who started his business by selling the spare parts he found in the trunk of a junked Packard; the Sussex County zookeeper who had a father-son relationship with the world's largest bear; the Thomas Edison–built concrete houses in Union and the remains of his concrete-production plant in Warren County; the ruined Stephen Crane Memorial in an overgrown vacant lot in Newark. I could— maybe should—fill a book with these stories—stories that got me infinitely fascinated with my home state.

In 1993, I did a series about the intercounty roads in the state. It was pure Jerseyana travel reportage, taking readers along the roads less traveled, following some old routes that began as Native American walking paths or colonial wagon routes.

It was an eight-part series, so at times I followed two connecting intercounty roads to develop a regional theme. (I cheated a little here, too, including sites not far from the chosen less-traveled road.)

I wanted to do a story on a Revolutionary War corridor so I picked a pair of roads, Routes 525 and 533, that basically connected the Morristown area with Trenton, via Somerville and Princeton.

I started at the beginning of Route 525, in Mendham, not far from Jockey Hollow. Not even a mile down the road, I made a discovery.

The First Presbyterian Church, known locally as the Hilltop Church, is a classic early American landmark with a 130-foot landmark steeple that towers over the surrounding hills. Buried behind the church are twenty-seven Revolutionary War soldiers who died at Jockey Hollow during a smallpox epidemic in 1777. The church was used as a sick bay during the epidemic. Buried along with the soldiers is the Reverend Thomas Lewis, the church pastor, who cared for the ailing men and died of the disease alongside them. Here was another good story. A local legend. I wondered how many others were out there.

Plenty.

That day alone I found out that a thirteen-star Betsy Ross flag flies perpetually over the Middlebrook Camp ground. That Washington plotted strategy for a frontier campaign against the Indians while headquartered at Somerville. That there is a monument in the front yard of a private home along the Millstone River that tells the story of the British raid that left Millstone, the colonial seat of Somerset County, burned to the ground. That the oak tree where Gen. Hugh Mercer lay mortally wounded still survives. That Richard Stockton, signer of the Declaration of Independence, is buried at the Friends Meeting House just south of the Princeton Battlefield. That a series of twelve markers follow the 11.8-mile route Washington took to Princeton after the two Battles of Trenton. These markers, one of which is buried deep in the woods and another of which sits in a farmer's cornfield, are mostly off Hamilton Avenue and Quaker Bridge Road through Trenton, Hamilton Township, Lawrence Township, and Princeton.

These discoveries made me realize how little I knew. I wanted to know more.

But when I began researching the Continental army's travels for the article, I was dismayed to find that not one readily available central source listed all New Jersey Revolutionary War sites.

Out of that disappointment came the idea for this book.

Until now, no single publication has listed detailed information about so many New Jersey Revolutionary sites. All previously published guides to the Revolution center on the highlights: Fort Lee and Washington's retreat across New Jersey; the victories at Trenton and Princeton; the brutal winter encampment at Jockey Hollow; and the Battle of Monmouth. Until now, there has not been much out there to help you fill in the blanks. You had to go out yourself and discover it.

I wanted to do that—to find and catalog as many Revolutionary War sites as possible. And so I began traveling the state, looking for the monuments, bronze plaques, and signs that mark our Revolutionary War history, as well as the private homes where history took place.

Armed with maps, pamphlets, outdated books (see the chapter titled "The Research," which contains full bibliographical references to all the print sources cited in this book), and a camera, I spent as much time on the road as I could, looking for Revolutionary War sites.

If you're out to discover New Jersey's Revolutionary trail from your car, almost any place called Washington is a good place to start.

On one side of New Jersey, the George Washington Bridge spans the Hudson River. On the other, Washington Crossing State Park overlooks the Delaware.

In between are six Washington Townships and a Washington Borough. You'll find a Washington Corner, a Washington Valley, and a pair of Washingtonvilles. There's a Washington Oak, a Washington Park, a Washington Place, and two Washington Rocks. There are towns or areas of towns named after the general in ten of New Jersey's twenty-one counties, and there are twenty-three major thoroughfares and hundreds of smaller ones throughout the state named Washington Avenue, Street, or Road. Not to mention the schools and parks.

Washington is a big name in New Jersey's geographic vernacular, and many places named after Washington are near places of some Revolutionary War significance.

Yes, Washington slept here . . . and lived here . . . and fought here. He crossed New Jersey in defeat, then crossed again in victory. Here he experienced what Thomas Paine, writing in Hackensack, characterized as "the times that try men's souls," and knew the elation of watching his ragtag army gel into a formidable fighting force. In all he spent nearly three years in New Jersey. He set up five longtime headquarters here in private homes: twice in Morristown, and once each in Somerville, Wayne, and Rocky Hill. In the last of these he wrote his final orders to his officers. He also stayed in dozens of other homes while traveling through the state.

At the foot of the George Washington Bridge is Fort Lee, which the Continental army abandoned in the face of a British rush that sent Washington into retreat across New Jersey. Washington Street in Morristown runs in front of the Ford Mansion, Washington's headquarters for the winter of 1779–80. Washington Avenue in Morristown heads out toward Jockey Hollow.

But even without the Washington clues, it's not hard to find Revolutionary War sites if you know how and where to look.

The most important thing to remember if you're exploring is that the main roads really haven't changed that much. Today's major highways mimic the paths of major routes in days of yore. For instance, six-lane Route 24 through the Hobart Gap in Summit took the place of a two-lane road, which replaced a dirt road as old as colonial days, which was based on a Lenni Lenape trail.

In some cases, the paths of the roads haven't changed at all. The Old York Road was the main road between New York and Philadelphia. Today you can pick that road up through Middlesex, Somerset, Hunterdon, western Monmouth, Mercer, and Burlington Counties. The Wallace House (Washington's headquarters in the winter of 1778–79), for example, is right off what was Old York Road.

Many parts of Route 202, which runs from Lambertville on a northeasterly slant up to Suffern, New York, were used during colonial times, as was Morris Avenue, connecting Elizabeth to Morristown. You'll find a good number of sites along or near these roads in towns that existed during colonial times.

As you explore, keep in mind that colonial towns were much more compact than today's. To find the old part of a town, for the most part, find the First Presbyterian Church. Even if the church building itself doesn't date back to colonial times it may well be on the site of the original, since the Presbyterians often rebuilt churches over the foundations of their old ones.

Churches today are often in town centers; in colonial times churches were the town centers. Most of the homes—especially those of influential people—were also close to the downtown areas. Areas where skirmishes took place were usually in the shadow of the church steeple.

Springfield is a great example of this. Every significant Revolutionary War site in town, including the Cannonball House and a D.A.R.–marked cemetery, is within a few hundred yards of the church.

You will also find that street names often correlate to sites. Beacon Road in Summit is right near the beacon site. The Caldwell Home in Union is on Caldwell Avenue. Peter Kemble's home in Harding Township is on Mt. Kemble Avenue (Route 202).

Of course, you can't just drive around aimlessly. I visited many local libraries and county historical societies to get started. In many cases, I interviewed the area authority—a person like Eric Olsen at Morristown

National Historical Park or John Mills at the Princeton Battlefield State Park—to uncover unlisted sites. So much is out there—much more than most of us ever knew.

There is a saying among collectors of rare things: "Behind each piece of a great collection is a great story."

The same can be said for many of the sites I have collected. There are great stories in the history of these places . . . that goes without saying. But there are also good stories in the preservation of these sites and in my personal discovery of them as well.

Three of my favorites are the home of famed spy John Honeyman in Griggstown, Gallows Hill in Westfield, and the home of Gen. David Forman in Manalapan.

Of the three, only the Honeyman house is listed in any previous publication—and without an exact address.

Honeyman was believed by his neighbors to be an ardent Loyalist, when in fact he was a great spy who reported directly to Washington (see the Griggstown section of the Somerset County chapter). During one exchange of information, Continental army troops pretended to imprison him, and even beat him up a little to make it convincing. Honeyman was so adept at infiltrating the British that, at war's end, Washington publicly commended him so that Honeyman and his family would be safe from revenge-minded Patriots.

I knew Honeyman's house was in the vicinity of the Griggstown village in the Delaware and Raritan Canal State Park. I stopped into the park office on the Griggstown causeway, but no one there had ever heard of Honeyman, let alone his house. I drove up and down Canal Road, just east of the Millstone River and the old Delaware and Raritan Canal. In trying to find the house, I made at least three passes, getting a clue from the name of one of the side streets, Bunker Hill Road (I figured maybe the area Patriots named it that long ago). In the immediate area there were a number of Revolutionary War–era homes, some on a scale grand enough to be worthy of a war hero. Before knocking on doors, I made one last pass, looking for a marker of some sort. Through a clearing in some high hedges, on a modest, one-story colonial home, I saw a hand-painted black-and-gold sign saying: "John Honeyman, Revolutionary War Spy and Patriot 1776–1786."

Gallows Hill in Westfield was a public execution place in colonial times. The most sensational hanging was that of an American sentry named James Morgan, who was convicted of murdering the popular rabble-rouser

James Caldwell in a dispute at Elizabethtown Point (see the Union section of the Union County chapter). Evidence surfaced at his trial that he had been paid by enemies of Caldwell to kill him should the chance arise.

I learned of this site from Robert Reynolds, who runs the Abraham Clark House, the headquarters of the Sons of the American Revolution. He said Morgan was hanged near the intersection of East Broad Street and Gallows Hill Road. I drove there to take a look around. Sure enough, embedded in the sidewalk was a plaque by the Westfield Bicentennial Commission marking the spot.

I learned of the General Forman house from Garry Stone, the historian at Monmouth Battlefield State Park. Forman had a checkered public life and at one point fended off accusations of profiteering. But he was best known for expunging Tory raiders and bandits from the Monmouth countryside. During the war, the county residents were hit often by these raiders from two directions: from Sandy Hook to the east and the Pine Barrens to the west. Washington asked Forman to take charge and he did with such overt force that he earned the nickname "Black David": many of the bandits (or suspected bandits) apprehended by Forman's men were executed with no questions asked.

The Forman house is not on any historic homes tour and is not marked. It is a small yellow house that sits in the most unlikely place—in the middle of the Covered Bridge condominium complex off Route 9 in Englishtown. The house is behind the condo association's clubhouse on Amberly Drive, the road that circles through the complex. It is surrounded by the pool and the tennis and bocce courts, and used for storage. It is in fairly good condition and in no danger of being taken down. That's the good news. The bad news is that there are also no plans to restore it or open it to the public.

In each case, the discovery was somewhat of a personal triumph. I was finding (and cataloging) things that very few people knew about. I was finding pieces of our state history, discovering New Jersey's Revolutionary War trail.

On one of my many trips around the state, I returned to Springfield. The shopping mall is still there, but the Newberry's is gone. I parked and got out of the car with my camera to take pictures of the Minuteman statue. As I worked, an older man came up and asked me what I was doing. I told him about this book and we talked about other sites in the area.

"Did you go to the cemetery?" he asked.

"The church cemetery?"

"No, the other one."

He told me that on the other side of the shopping mall was a small Revolutionary War burial ground. I know this area well, I told him, but I'd never noticed a cemetery.

"C'mon," he said. "I'll show you."

I walked with him down past the shopping mall. Just beyond it, next to the small commercial building at 37 Mountain Avenue, was a patch of land elevated above the sidewalk and hidden by shrubs and trees. The steps leading up to it were missing an iron railing. The cemetery contains maybe twenty-five grave markers, a few of which display the names of Continental army soldiers. Two plaques there—placed by the Sons of the American Revolution and the Daughters of the Revolution—indicate that there are a number of unmarked graves of soldiers killed during the fighting on June 23, 1780.

New Jersey's Revolutionary War history is an undervalued commodity. The state does little to promote it, and our schools do little to teach it.

While states like Massachusetts, Pennsylvania, and Virginia trumpet their glorious patriotic pasts, New Jersey sits subdued, like the stereotypical sullen, contemplative war hero at the end of the bar.

It's a shame.

The Revolution shows up nowhere in the state motto or on specialty license plates. State tourism campaigns are aimed to lure people to the Shore. The tourism motto, "New Jersey and You, Perfect Together," certainly does nothing to tell out-of-staters of our rich colonial past.

There has only been one major campaign that emphasized the Revolutionary War theme for New Jersey tourism. That was before the nation's 1976 Bicentennial celebration, but the fervor died down right after the milestone date passed.

A second campaign was launched in 1998. The centerpiece of the campaign was a glossy twelve-page booklet called *A Revolutionary Time.* The booklet was developed not by the State Office of Travel and Tourism but by the State Division of Parks and Forestry. It is a slick, informative booklet, but it is strictly an in-state campaign, not aimed at out-of-state tourists.

It's hard to understand why we don't play up our history. It's hard to understand why we Jerseyans are bashful about proclaiming our greatness . . . about taking our rightful place among the states that formed this nation politically . . . militarily . . . socially . . . and economically.

A few years ago, I heard a New York State radio ad campaign targeted at out-of-state tourists and promoting the historical wonders of the Empire State. The commercial, narrated by *Civil War* filmmaker Ken Burns, mentioned the Revolutionary War battlefield at Saratoga, the birthplace of the woman suffrage movement at Seneca Falls, and Cooperstown, home of the baseball Hall of Fame.

Immediately I thought, "Yeah, and in New Jersey we have the Monmouth battlefield, the Botto House, home of the American labor movement, and Hoboken, the birthplace of baseball."

What we don't have is a media campaign to promote all of it.

What we need is a major campaign to educate Jerseyans and other Americans about New Jersey history.

What we need is a snappy, telling motto like . . . "Do Something Revolutionary, Visit New Jersey."

Now that would be perfect.

But promotion of New Jersey historical sites only solves part of the problem.

We also need to teach our kids more about significant local history. Right now, our schools teach New Jersey history in fourth grade . . . one skinny year to learn about everything from the migrations of the Lenni Lenape to Washington's surprise attack at Trenton to Thomas Edison's inventions to the suburban sprawl of the last half of the twentieth century. When kids later learn about the American Revolution, they're taught from books that do not emphasize New Jersey's role.

We have taught generations of New Jersey kids about the Boston Tea Party but not the Greenwich tea burning . . . about the miserable winter at Valley Forge but not Jockey Hollow . . . we have taken our kids on class trips to the Philadelphia's Independence Hall but not Princeton's Nassau Hall.

Local history is almost never emphasized.

I grew up in Summit, which overlooks Springfield, home of the war's last major encounter in New Jersey. I never learned about the strategic importance of Hobart Gap (about a mile from my house), or why Beacon Hill was named such (it housed one of the Lord Stirling–designed fire tower warning beacons). The beacon was at what today is 226 Hobart Avenue. Next to it was a cannon nicknamed "Old Sow." Prior to the Battle of Springfield, Old Sow boomed out to bring the militiamen out of the mountains to take on the British. A great local legend . . . not taught in Summit public schools. Not then, not now.

Mrs. Ranell Shea, the current owner of 226 Hobart Avenue, said she contacted the schools to tell them of the property's significance.

"They were surprised," she said. "They said, 'We should come up there for a field trip,' but they never did."

Over in Madison, which has another highly regarded school system, my older two children would walk past the Sayre House—where Mad Anthony Wayne stayed during one of the Continental army's Morristown encampments—every day. The children would pass this house, then get to school and learn about things that happened in other places.

Some might argue that teaching local history is too parochial, that it offers too narrow a view. Not so.

Take the case of the Watchungs. Washington spent much of the war in and around these mountains, setting up headquarters and encampments at Wayne, Morristown, and Somerville. The lay of the Watchungs gave him vantage points to the south and east (where the British were entrenched), escape routes to the north and west, access to food and other provisions from the West Jersey farmlands, and most important, protection from quick strikes. If you understand Washington in the Watchungs, you begin to appreciate his genius not only as a military strategist but as a surveyor as well.

He exploited the British ignorance of the landscape and always positioned himself on higher ground. Instead of fighting for the cities, he took the mountains by default and bought time . . . time to regroup and heal, time to drum up new recruits, time to procure provisions, and time to get Congress to fund the war, knowing the home team almost always wins a war of attrition. By holding down the Watchungs, he made it impossible for the British to cut the colonies in half—they never truly had command of the Mid-Atlantic Region.

Now take the case of the Battle of Springfield.

For three weeks in June 1780, the British force led by the German general Wilhelm von Knyphausen pounded Elizabethtown (now Elizabeth), Connecticut Farms (now Union), and Springfield. The British plan was to race through the Watchung Mountain gap at Summit and Short Hills to attack Gen. George Washington at Morristown.

That was the military agenda. But there was a political agenda, too.

Most school kids think the American Revolution was a war between the colonies and England. Forgotten in this simplistic teaching is that the war also pitted neighbor against neighbor—it was part revolution and part civil war. Many Americans didn't want independence. They wanted to remain British subjects. These people were known as Loyalists and Tories, and the area around Springfield was a hotbed of pro-British activity.

When Knyphausen's troops arrived in Elizabethtown, they immediately went on a muscle-flexing campaign designed to make those who wanted independence think twice about their choice, and to give Loyalists a feeling of confidence in their king.

In the weeks leading up to the battle, the British burned churches and public buildings in Elizabethtown and Connecticut Farms. But at Connecticut Farms, their plan to intimidate the revolutionaries backfired.

During the fighting, Hannah Caldwell, the wife of James Caldwell, was shot and killed in the kitchen of her home in front of her children. Word spread that she had been purposely murdered by a British soldier, although it has never been proven.

But one thing is certain: The incident became one of the most notorious atrocities of the entire war. The alleged murder of Hannah Caldwell by the redcoats helped rally New Jerseyans against the invaders. After being held at Springfield, the British left New Jersey, obviously aware that their support here was waning.

See how a little insight into the Battle of Springfield gives you a much greater understanding of the political climate in America.

See how far a little local history goes.

The Battle of Springfield was a heroic episode, especially for the New Jersey militia. They dug in and turned back a force of six thousand British regulars and, in essence, booted England out of New Jersey.

In Virginia or Massachusetts or Pennsylvania or any other state that commercially extols its Revolutionary War history, the battlefield at Springfield would be hallowed ground. It would today be a tourist attraction with a park, some monuments, weekly reenactments, T-shirt sales, and an interpretive center with one of those narrated electronic maps explaining troop movements.

But this is New Jersey and part of the battleground became a downtown strip mall—a good example of how our commercial development has devastated our historic-site stockpile.

Architectural historians estimate that only 5 percent of what stood in the eighteenth century is standing today. But when you consider that most of the New Jersey Revolutionary War activity happened in what was then—and what is now—the busy New York–Philadelphia corridor, it's easy to see why so much been destroyed.

New Jersey has been fortunate to have a vibrant manufacturing and retail economy. The development of the New York–Philadelphia corridor has accelerated in this century and, with money to be made, historic preservation has often been overlooked.

The strong economy hurt historic preservation in another way. The availability of jobs brings a certain transient population, native and immigrant, to the state. There are very few of us with great-great-great grandfathers in the local cemetery. In America's slower-paced and rural areas, there are multigenerational, bloodline caretakers of local history. In New Jersey, we grow fast, we come and go, we trample things that were important to the previous generation.

Despite all this, there is still a lot to see in New Jersey. And that's what this book is all about. Yes, this book is about history, but more than anything else, it's a road adventure. It's a book about exploring the cities and countryside, finding the roadside markers and the forgotten plaques that tell us something happened here. Our history is out there—in our busy cities and rural towns, in our public historic sites and in private homes, in fading historical society markers and cemetery memorials.

To find the history in New Jersey, you can't rely on the state or the education system to show you the way. You have to get out there and discover it yourself. For you and your children or grandchildren.

Our kids live in a world where they are bombarded by pop culture . . . music, TV, movies, sports. History can only compete for a place in their consciousness if we keep history interesting . . . if we tell real stories about real people and find the real places near our homes. We need to let the kids make history theirs. To let them see the human element in the Washingtons and the Edisons, to see the places they worked and walked. History should not be stuffy . . . it should be the smells from the working colonial kitchen at Rockingham . . . the cannon fire outside the Old Barracks at Trenton . . . the great living oak in the meadow where Gen. Hugh Mercer lay dying . . . the thundering Passaic falls Alexander Hamilton harnessed for industry . . . the elegance of the Llewellyn Park mansion where Thomas Edison finally reclined . . . the blinding beams of our towering lighthouses . . . the pastel gentility of Cape May, Ocean Grove, and Mt. Tabor.

The only way for history to compete is to be relevant, not distant.

And believe it or not, it's as close as your own neighborhood.

Bergen County

New Jersey got its first taste of major Revolutionary War activity in November 1776, when the British began chasing the Continental army across the state.

Washington's retreat across New Jersey, which began in Bergen County, was the culmination of a major British initiative to seize New York.

After the British took Boston, Washington looked to defend New York and the Hudson River Valley. The British, of course, had other ideas. They wanted to put a quick end to the uprising by controlling the Hudson and cutting the colonies in half. King George III sent thousands of men to America in the largest armed fleet ever to sail out of England. Including Hessians and American Loyalists, the king's army numbered about thirty-one thousand as it gathered on Staten Island. The British crossed into Gravesend in Brooklyn and drove the Americans north into Manhattan during the Battle of Long Island (actually Brooklyn) on August 27, 1776. Three weeks later, they drove the Americans out of Manhattan in the Battle of Harlem Heights. On October 28, Gen. William Howe defeated Washington at White Plains. Washington retreated, crossed the Hudson at Peekskill, and entered New Jersey through Bergen County, following the bank of the Hackensack River. Howe turned south and headed toward Fort Washington, across the Hudson from Fort Lee.

Washington had hoped these forts, which commanded heights over the river, would keep the British Navy from sailing up the Hudson. But both forts were overrun in a matter of days. Fort Washington fell first, on

November 16, surrendered by Col. Robert Magaw after an invading force of more than six thousand men overwhelmed his force of twenty-nine hundred. Four days later, Fort Lee fell, and the British began their perplexingly casual pursuit of Washington across North Jersey.

Over the next few years, Bergen County was in the middle of the grappling for control of the area by both sides. Adrian C. Leiby's book *The Revolutionary War in the Hackensack Valley* (see the Research chapter) does an excellent job of documenting troop movement and skirmishes, with a large number of maps to help you generalize locations. The book also details the suffering of the residents: both armies circulated among the farms and continually pillaged them of livestock, and neighbor turned against neighbor as sympathies fluctuated between the cause and the Crown.

This pillaging was a major concern of Washington's. As he drew his army closer and closer to British points in New York during the summer of 1780, he had this to say to his troops:

> The Army now being near the enemy, the Gen'l flatters himself [to think] every Officer and Soldier will make it a point of Honor . . . to be at the shortest notice ready to Act as circumstances may require . . . should an opportunity be afforded us that every part of the Army will vie with each other and display the conduct, fortitude and bravery which ought to distinguish troops fighting for their Country, their Liberty, for everything dear to the Citizen or to the Soldier. He also hopes to hear of no wanton depredation on the persons or property of the Inhabitants.

 Alpine

The Blackledge-Kearney House at Closter's Landing
Palisades Interstate Park (follow signs to Alpine Boat Basin)
(201) 768-1360 or (201) 461-1776
HOURS: Saturday and Sunday, noon to 5 P.M. Open only in April, May, September, and October.

The British army, led by Gen. Charles Cornwallis, began landing in force in New Jersey in the early morning of November 20. About six thousand soldiers came ashore at Closter's Landing, across the river from modern-day Yonkers, and began climbing the steep trails of the Palisades before marching six miles south to attack Fort Lee (then known as Fort Constitution). Legend has it that Cornwallis stopped in at the Blackledge-Kearney House— an inn for boatmen and river travelers of the day—and had tea with his officers. Thanks to this brief layover, the house came to be called "Cornwallis

Headquarters," as a plaque outside states. Later in the day, Cornwallis, too, made the climb and led his force to Fort Lee, which he found had been quickly abandoned.

The Closter's Landing area is in the vicinity of the house, including where a yacht club stands today. North of the house is a big picnic area with rustic furniture and rock walls.

The scenery alone is worth the trip. Rest stops along the Palisades Parkway offer dramatic views of New York City. To reach Closter's Landing, you must get off the parkway and drive along the Henry Hudson Parkway, which descends to the base of the cliffs near the river's edge. The house is at the end of that road, just beyond a park maintenance garage.

Englewood

Liberty Pole
Corner of Lafayette and Palisade Avenues

One of the first Liberty Poles to go up in New Jersey was here. Local folks raised this public symbol of American defiance to celebrate the repeal of the Stamp Act in 1766. Near the intersection was a well-trafficked tavern, which was the site of a skirmish between Col. "Light-Horse" Harry Lee's men and local Loyalists after Lee raided Paulus Hook (in what is now Jersey City).

There are thirteen other documented skirmishes in this area, which was politically split between Patriots and Loyalists. An area that today is Cliffside Park, Englewood, Englewood Cliffs, Leonia, and Fort Lee was known then as "English Neighborhood." It was here that most of the action took place, including fierce battles on October 19, 1776, and November 9, 1776, which resulted in dozens of casualties on both sides.

Fort Lee

Fort Lee Historic Park
Hudson Terrace
(201) 461-1776
HOURS: Wednesday through Sunday, 10 A.M. to 5 P.M.

The first thing any traveler should know about the Fort Lee Historic Park is that, in some ways, it is difficult to find. Unlike major historic areas like Washington's Headquarters (The Ford Mansion) at Morristown National Historical Park, and Washington Crossing State Park, there are no signs on major roads directing you to the park. And once you get lost, you can find yourself in a myriad of one-way streets that suddenly become highway entrances: one false move and you could be jettisoned out to Route 80 or 46 West, or worse, over the George Washington Bridge.

The bridge, however, is the key to finding the park. The park lies directly south of the bridge, where Main Street meets Hudson Terrace. If you find yourself crossing under the bridge (south to north), you know you've gone too far.

The bridge is also key to one of the best features of the park—you can't beat the New York City views from its Palisades perch. In the picnic area north of the visitors' center, you can look toward New York City from almost directly underneath the road surface of the 3,500-foot span and gain an appreciation of the magnitude of the bridge as an engineering feat. The eastern tower is 680 feet high—twice as high as the cliff you are standing on. As you walk through the park there are a number of scenic overlooks which give you overwhelming southward views of the Hudson River as it cuts through the canyon formed by Manhattan skyscrapers rising on the east banks and high-rise apartment buildings on the Jersey side. It is simply an awe-inspiring sight, like a man-made Grand Canyon.

It is easy to understand why Washington, a trained surveyor, picked this spot to defend the Hudson. It is high enough to see any fleet movement developing in either Upper or Lower New York Bay (especially in the days when there were no buildings over three stories high except for church steeples). And it is close enough to the river to shell passing ships. With a twin fort (Fort Washington) across the river, Washington hoped to make the Hudson impenetrable.

Unfortunately for the Americans, all the thought that went into the planning and all the hard work that went into building the gun batteries on the cliffs didn't matter when the British overran Fort Washington on November 16, 1776, while Washington watched from Fort Lee. On November 20, Cornwallis landed six miles north of the fort with six thousand men flush from a number of victories in New York and marched south.

In the *Encyclopedia of the American Revolution* (see the Research chapter), Col. Mark Boatner III describes the scene like this:

> The British found two or three hundred tents still standing and pots still boiling. Twelve drunken Americans were captured in the fort, and about a hundred fifty other prisoners were taken in the vicinity. Although the Americans had managed to evacuate stocks of gunpowder, they left behind a thousand barrels of flour, all their entrenching tools, about fifty cannon, and their baggage.

By sacrificing this matériel, however, Washington had led two thousand troops from the fort to safety before the British could seize the one bridge across the Hackensack River.

Thus began Washington's retreat across New Jersey, certainly the low point of the war for the Americans. The Washington retreat route loosely follows what today is Fort Lee Road to Grand Avenue in Leonia, to Palisades Avenue in Englewood, up Lafayette to Liberty Road to Washington Avenue in Bergenfield to New Bridge Road (see the River Edge section of this chapter). There were a large number of road signs marking this route at the time of the Bicentennial but many are gone now.

The visitors' center at Fort Lee Historic Park is among the top three information stops in the state—the other two being the museum at the Ford Mansion at Morristown National Historical Park (see the Morris County chapter) and the visitors' center at Washington Crossing State Park (see the Mercer County chapter). There are exhibits on uniforms and weaponry, and a time line about the battle for New York City and Washington's retreat.

In the fall, it is not unusual to see school groups in the replica camp area south of the visitors' center being drilled like Continental soldiers as part of the park's living history program.

Garfield

Post Ford Monument
River Road and Columbus Avenue

On a small rise that juts out into the fast-moving Passaic River is a five-foot-tall fieldstone monument. A hand-painted inscription says, "Post Ford, used by both American and British Armies during the Revolution."

During the retreat from Fort Lee, Washington and his army passed this way before crossing the Passaic at Acquackanonk Bridge (see the Wallington section of this chapter).

Hackensack

The Green
Intersection of Washington Place and Court, Green, and Main Streets.

At the center of this intersection is a monument to Gen. Enoch Poor, a New Hampshire brigade commander who was one of the heroes of the Battle of

Saratoga in the fall of 1777. He died of a fever near Hackensack three years later and is buried across the street in the Dutch Reformed Church cemetery. Washington and the Marquis de Lafayette were among the dignitaries at Poor's full military funeral. Poor was in the area because Washington had amassed an army there for a planned attack on New York City (which never materialized).

Across the street, at the northeast corner of Main Street and Washington Place, is the site of the Mansion House, the home of Judge Peter Zabriskie, the leading citizen of Hackensack and a staunch patriot. Zabriskie was one of the driving forces in Bergen County politics and a founder of Queen's College (Rutgers). Washington was a frequent visitor at the house and stayed a night during the retreat of 1776. On a Bergen County map of Revolutionary War sites done for the Bicentennial, the Zabriskie house site is noted as a "Washington's Headquarters." He was there when he learned of the planned British attack on Fort Washington, and he rode to Fort Lee on horseback to appraise the situation. He headquartered there when the British landed at Closter's Landing and he decided to abandon Fort Lee.

The Mansion House later became a small hotel, first known as the Albany Stage Coach and then the Madison House. Room 19 was known to be Washington's room. Unfortunately, the building was torn down in 1945 and a commercial building with law offices and a bail bondsman's office sits on the spot.

On the west side of the green is a historical marker on the location of the second Bergen County Courthouse, which was burned to the ground by marauding British and Hessian patrols on the night of March 23, 1780.

Ho-ho-kus

The Hermitage
335 North Franklin Turnpike
(201) 445-8311
HOURS: Wednesdays, 1 P.M. to 4 P.M., and two Sundays a month,
      1 P.M. to 4 P.M. Call for exact dates.

During colonial times, the large brownstone house with the gabled roof was owned by a British officer, Lt. Col. James Marcus Prevost, who died before the Revolution. His widow, Theodosia, liked to entertain influential people, especially military men. She eventually married Aaron Burr, at the time a colonel in the Continental army. It is believed that Washington stayed here for a few days in July 1778, and the house is marked as a "Washington's Headquarters" on the Bergen County Bicentennial map.

The house is now operated by the nonprofit Friends of Hermitage as a historical museum with an emphasis on the Victorian era.

Oakland

The Hendrick Van Allen House
Corner of Route 202 and Franklin Avenue
(201) 825-9049
HOURS: First and third Sunday of each month, 1 P.M. to 4 P.M.
Closed in July and August, December and January.

This house, now owned by the Oakland Historical Society, is a squat stone structure that was used by Washington on the days of July 14 and 15, 1777, while he moved troops from Morristown north to New York.

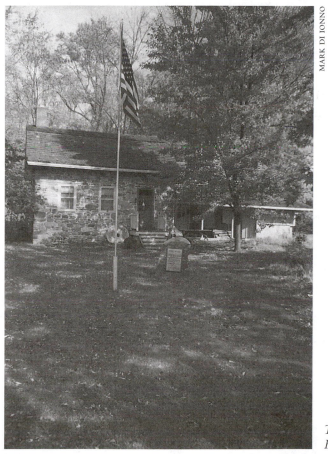

MARK DI IONNO

The Hendrick Van Allen House

Paramus

Zabriskie Mills Site
Red Mill Road, South of Route 4

When British and Hessian troops attacked Hackensack on March 23, 1780, they captured nearly all the men in town and jailed them briefly at Zabriskie Mills. The site today is called Easton Tower Historic Site. It became the home of Edward D. Easton, a recording industry pioneer. In 1899, he built the existing waterwheel and stone tower that is now the centerpiece of the park.

Washington Spring Garden Historic Site
Van Saun County Park
Corner of Forest and Howland Avenues

From September 4 through September 20, 1780, Washington's army camped at an area known as Steenrapie, which stretched along Kinderkamack Road toward Emerson. This was a major encampment with troops and a thirty-gun artillery unit, amassing along both sides of Kinderkamack Road for two miles in the River Edge–Hackensack area, and into the area of Van Saun Park. The army was there as Washington debated an all-out attack on Manhattan. The spring at Van Saun Park was used for the troops' water supply. Washington is said to have drunk from the spring on September 13, when he played host to six local Indian chiefs, who trailed behind him while he reviewed the troops. The spring is between areas M and L of the park.

 Ridgefield

English Neighborhood Reformed Church
1040 Edgewater Avenue
(201) 943-1231

The English Neighborhood Reformed Church was moved, stone by stone, from the old English Neighborhood after the war to the current site. The pastor during the war was a renowned Tory, and had to abandon the pulpit for England when the war heated up. At the first site, at Grand and Hillside Avenues in Leonia, is a plaque commemorating the old church.

River Edge

Historic New Bridge Landing Park
End of Main Street. (Main Street intersects with Hackensack
    Avenue about a mile north of Route 4. Turn right on Main
    Street into New Bridge complex.)

(201) 487-1739

HOURS: Wednesday through Saturday, 10 A.M. to noon and 1 P.M. to 5 P.M.

The two thousand soldiers and officers who evacuated Fort Lee were basically in a foot race with Cornwallis's army to get across the Hackensack. On the cold and rainy night of November 20, 1776—just five months after the Continental Congress had boldly put forth its Declaration of Independence—they won that race and crossed the Hackensack River at New Bridge.

Washington's army had been all but defeated. It had suffered enormous casualties and loss of captives to Howe's skilled soldiers at the Battles of Long Island, Harlem Heights, White Plains, and Fort Washington. Now it was in full-gallop retreat, without the tents and other supplies lost at Fort Lee.

It was the conditions at New Bridge that inspired Thomas Paine to write *The Crisis*, which began with the famous line, "These are the times that try men's souls."

Whether Paine began writing here or at Military Park in Newark is a matter of historical dispute (see the Newark section of the Essex and Hudson Counties chapter).

But Washington readjusted his war strategy here. It was no longer about victory in combat, it was about survival and attrition. It was not about winning, it was about not surrendering. In correspondence from Bergen County, Washington said that the British would have difficulty feeding their huge army on the run; that hunger for both sides would work in his favor. His actions from here on in were always about keeping his manpower up and engaging his army only in less risky conflict. Six weeks later, he would surprise the Hessians at Trenton and then hit the British at Princeton, but in each case he would avoid major full-scale confrontation with the British regulars.

But that was later. On November 20, as the cold and weary rebels headed toward the Hackensack at New Bridge, local Tories were begging the British to move quickly and take control of the bridges. They wanted the American army trapped between the Hackensack and Hudson Rivers, with Newark Bay at the south. But General Howe had other ideas, including a meeting with Cornwallis in which he formally bestowed congratulations for routing Fort Lee. Cornwallis is often blamed for the casualness of the pursuit of Washington but, in fact, the responsibility was Howe's. Howe wanted a political resolution to the conflict. He did not want it to end by chasing a ragtag bunch of retreaters into a chaotic mutiny. Cornwallis was an aggressive soldier and wanted to deliver the killer blow. Howe ordered him to chase Washington no further south than New Brunswick.

At New Bridge Landing Park are five buildings, including the Steuben House, which belonged to Jan Zabriskie, a Loyalist who was arrested in 1777 and had his home confiscated in 1780. Washington stayed here September 4, 1780, while his army settled in at Steenrapie. Before that, the British had been guests here, too. No house in America was used so often by both sides.

In 1783, the state gave the Zabriskie house and property to a Prussian officer, Baron Frederick William von Steuben, who had volunteered for the American cause. He was responsible for putting professional soldiering into the Continental army, beginning with military training at Valley Forge. The house today is an example of Jersey Dutch architecture and furnishing. Other attractions at the site include the Demarest House Museum, the Campbell-Christie House, and an authentic colonial kitchen in a separate outbuilding.

River Vale

Baylor Massacre Park
Red Oak Drive (near junction of River Vale Road)

On the night of September 27, 1778, Col. George Baylor and his 152 officers and soldiers of Virginia's Third Regiment Light Dragoons settled in for the night in barns owned by Cornelius Haring along what was then called Overkill Road (now River Vale Road). In the middle of the night, they were attacked by a force led by Maj. Gen. Charles Grey, a British officer with a reputation for night-time ambushes.

Grey was led to the sleeping regiment by local Tories. In the fighting, between six and eleven Americans were killed immediately and about seventy were injured. Baylor's second in command, Maj. Alexander Clough, died a few days later of injuries sustained in the fighting. Baylor survived, but injuries he received contributed to his death a few years later.

The men were buried the next day in tanning vats on the property by the Bergen militia and the site was marked by a large round millstone. In the 1960s, an archaeological study was ordered to confirm the existence of the graves and six bodies were found. A county park was built around the site in 1972 as a memorial.

Wallington

Acquackanonk Bridge
Corner of Main and Passaic Streets

As Washington and his army retreated from Fort Lee through the Hackensack Valley, they crossed the Passaic River over the Acquackanonk Bridge on November 21, 1776, and burned it behind them. The army stayed in Passaic, then known as Acquackanonk, for a night before moving south toward Newark. (Note: The blue-and-silver plaque on the Wallington side of the current bridge gives the wrong year for the crossing. It says November 21, 1777.)

Burlington County

The state's biggest county at over eight hundred square miles, Burlington was even bigger during the early colonial days. The state's first county was enormous and included parts of what today are Mercer, Hunterdon, Morris, Sussex, Warren, and Ocean Counties. In short, it dominated West Jersey. It was the first county to put in a county government and courts. In 1676, the Proprietors of West Jersey issued the Concessions and Agreements, which guaranteed freedom of speech and religion and the right to a trial by jury—13 years before the English Bill of Rights and 113 years before the adoption of the U.S. Constitution. The Proprietors in 1676 also formally objected to "taxation without representation"—they were among the first colonists to do so. That document, written in part by William Penn, is stored at the surveyor general's office on West Broad Street in Burlington (city).

By the time of the Revolution the county had been reduced in size, but it was prosperous and no less interested in independence. There were a number of prominent Loyalists—including Royal Governor William Franklin, the son of Benjamin Franklin; Burlington Mayor John Lawrence; and St. Mary's Church pastor Jonathan Odell. But the vocal Patriots, led by Francis Hopkinson, made it clear that those loyal to the crown risked incarceration. In fact, Lawrence was jailed and both Franklin and Odell left America for England.

There were few significant battles in the county and fighting between Loyalists and Patriots was probably kept to a minimum due to the over-

whelming presence of the pacifist Quakers—unlike places like Union and Bergen counties, where neighbors harassed neighbors throughout the war.

The bulk of the British army marched through the county in June 1778, when the commander in chief, Gen. Henry Clinton, evacuated Philadelphia and marched through New Jersey to the Raritan Bay to reach New York. He was intercepted at Monmouth Court House by Washington and the Battle of Monmouth took place.

As the British troops moved through the area, they split into two columns at what is today the junction of Routes 70 and 41 (Kings Highway) in Haddonfield (see the Lower Delaware chapter), before rejoining at Mount Holly. Clinton sent the Hessians under General von Knyphausen north along Kings Highway into Moorestown, while he took his troops into Mount Laurel. The invaders forced the Burlington County residents to provide hospitality, commandeering homes and stealing not only food but almost everything else they could get their hands on.

Beverly

Dunk's Ferry Marker
End of Cooper Street

As part of his planned Christmas attack on the Hessians at Trenton, Washington wanted Gen. John Cadwalader of the Pennsylvania militia to cross the Delaware south of Trenton and land at Duncan Williamson's Ferry (Dunk's Ferry) to attack the Hessians at Bordentown. The weather, however, prevented Cadwalader from crossing. A marker at the flagpole here tells the story.

Bordentown

Thomas Paine Home
Corner of Farnsworth and East Church Street
(Private)

Thomas Paine's *Common Sense* was a forty-seven-page pamphlet that cost two shillings when it began selling on the streets of Philadelphia in January 1776. Three months later, 120,000 copies had been sold, and thirty-nine-year-old Thomas Paine—son of a poor corset maker and a self-educated failure at every occupation he had tried—became the plain-speaking voice of the revolutionary cause.

Common Sense was followed by *The Crisis,* which Paine wrote while traveling with the Continental army during Washington's retreat across New Jersey:

> These are the times that try men's souls. The summer soldier and sun-shine patriot will, in this crisis, shrink from the service of their country; but he that stands it now deserves the love and thanks of man and woman. Tyranny, like hell, is not easily conquered; yet we have this consolation with us, that the harder the conflict, the more glorious the triumph.

Paine was hired by Congress to be the secretary to the committee on foreign affairs, but had a checkered career in government. He was forced to resign after a flap with the French government, but was also influential in helping Congress get money and supplies from the French in 1781.

He moved to Bordentown in 1783 and stayed until 1789, when he left for Europe to get financing for his invention, the iron bridge, which turned out to be an engineering success, but financially impractical. He also threw himself (and his writings) into the French Revolution. But he missed home. In one letter he wrote, "My heart and myself are three thousand miles apart; and I had rather see my horse, Button, eating the grass of Bordentown than see all the show and pomp of Europe."

The writer who inspired the Revolution was now beginning to irritate the folks back home. *The Age of Reason* (1794) attacked organized religion, a staple of American life. Worse, his "Letter to George Washington" (1796) attacked not only Washington's policies as president but his military record as well. He returned to Bordentown in 1802, but found that his old friends were no longer so friendly and was literally run out of town.

The Paine house today, believe it or not, is a dentist's office. A small bronze plaque tells of the building's historical significance.

Colonel Joseph Borden Home
32 Farnsworth Avenue
(Private)

Borden was the transportation entrepreneur for whom the town was named. With his backing, Patriots from Bordentown launched a number of float-ing kegs filled with gunpowder into the Delaware in January 1778, hoping they would strike the British fleet anchored in the river off Philadelphia. One keg struck, killing four British sailors. In May the British sailed to Borden-town in five armed ships and twenty flat-bottomed boats, landing eight hun-dred soldiers. Borden's house was burned to the ground (and rebuilt soon after). Legend has it that as Mrs. Borden watched the house go up in flames, a British officer apologized.

"This is the happiest day of my life," she replied. "I know you have given up all hope of reconquering my country, or you would not thus wantonly devastate it."

The Hopkinson House
101 Farnsworth (corner of Park and Farnsworth)
(Private)

Francis Hopkinson was a signer of the Declaration of Independence and a son-in-law of the town's most prominent citizen, Col. Joseph Borden. Hopkinson had an eclectic career. He was the first graduate of the University of Pennsylvania, a political satirist, a Congressional delegate, and a designer of government who claimed to have been the artistic brains behind the Stars and Stripes. After the floating powder keg incident, he wrote a twenty-two-verse ditty called *The Battle of the Kegs*, which became a popular hit in the colonies. One verse, in particular, gave British-haters joy:

> Sir William he, snug as a flea
> Lay all this time a snoring;
> Nor dream'd of harm, as he lay warm
> In bed with Mrs. L———.

The American House Site
(A Colonial Tavern)
135 E. Park Street

This was the site of a revolutionary-era tavern owned by Col. Oakly Hoagland of the Continental army. It was a popular gathering spot of the patriotic-minded, but also the headquarters for Col. Kurt von Donop, who commanded two thousand Hessians stationed there. Von Donop was lured out of Bordentown by reports that the Americans were amassing a force of three thousand to march north from Mount Holly. He wanted to avoid being trapped against the river in a fight against a stronger force and also wanted to head off the American march. He took his men to Mount Holly, where he encountered a force of only six hundred in the Battle of Iron Works Hill (see the Mount Holly section of this chapter).

Military historians say that had von Donop stayed in Bordentown, he would have been readily available to help the Hessians in Trenton three days later. Instead, Washington stormed the city, and the rest is history.

Burlington

John Lawrence House
459 High Street
(Private)

Lawrence, the mayor of Burlington at the time of the Revolution, had strong ties to England and entertained Hessian officers at his home. He was eventually jailed for his pro-Crown activities.

Old St. Mary's Church
Corner of Wood and Broad Streets

The Reverend Jonathan Odell was another big fan of King George III, and used his pulpit to promote Loyalist activities. Burlington County Patriots literally ran him out of town on one occasion, and he sailed to safety in England.

Site of Royal Governor's Mansion
Riverbank
Off West Delaware Avenue between Talbot and Wood Streets

Here at the site of the Veterans of Foreign Wars Hall was the New Jersey royal governor's mansion, last occupied by William Franklin, the son of Benjamin Franklin. As further evidence that the American Revolution was very much a civil war that divided families, William Franklin was an ardent Loyalist, while his father helped draft, and signed, the Declaration of Independence. William Franklin was imprisoned in his mansion by local revolutionaries, then moved to England and never returned. Benjamin Franklin is one of the enduring figures from the early days of American independence, the only nonpresident on our currency. There is a historical marker on this site.

East on West Delaware at High Street is the spot where the British frigates involved in the attack on Bordentown shelled the Burlington wharf on their way back down the Delaware to Philadelphia. According to legend, British sailors warned two boys and their dogs to get away from the area before they began the bombardment.

New-Jersey Gazette Site
206 High Street

It was here that Benjamin Franklin printed New Jersey's first currency in 1728, and almost fifty years later Isaac Collins printed the state's first newspaper, the New-Jersey Gazette, on December 5, 1777. While Collins wasn't as pro-Patriot as his North Jersey counterpart Shepard Kollock (see the Chatham section of the Morris County chapter), he had a reputation for honesty in evaluating the political situation. Collins's house is four blocks away at the corner of East Broad Street and York Avenue. Temple B'nai Israel at 212 High Street, built in 1916, is one of the oldest synagogues in South Jersey.

The Boudinot-Bradford House
207 Broad Street
(Private)

Elias Boudinot came to Burlington toward the end of his distinguished career (see the Elizabeth section of the Union County chapter), during which he served as president of the Continental Congress. William Bradford, Boudinot's son-in-law, was the second attorney general under George Washington. The house now is in considerable disrepair.

Boudinot is buried at (new) St. Mary's Church at 145 West Broad Street, as are Joshua Wallace, a delegate to the New Jersey convention that ratified the U.S. Constitution, and Joseph Bloomfield, a captain in the Revolution and an early governor of New Jersey.

Blue Anchor Inn
Site of Blue Anchor Tavern
Corner of High and Broad Streets

The current building, constructed in 1856, is in disrepair. The Blue Anchor Tavern was established in 1750 and was one of the most popular gathering places in South Jersey. British and American troops used it during the war.

Crosswicks

Friends Meeting House
Church Street
(609) 298-4362

The little Quaker village of Crosswicks in northwestern Burlington County was a stopping point for Gen. Henry Clinton's army as it marched across New Jersey after evacuating Philadelphia on its way to the Raritan Bay. But before being intercepted by Washington's full force at Monmouth (see the Shore Counties chapter), the British were harassed by American units under Col. Elias Dayton. On June 23, 1778—five days before the big battle at Monmouth—American troops tried to burn the bridge at Crosswicks Creek, leading to a skirmish in the village. It is said that Dayton had his horse shot out from underneath him during the fighting. Also during the fighting, three cannonballs struck the Friends Meeting House, where Clinton's army was centered. One lodged in the north wall, and remains there today.

That skirmish was not the first action the Meeting House saw in the Revolution. In December 1776, the Americans under Col. Silas Newcomb used it as a headquarters before the second Battle of Trenton.

Hainesport

Route 537 Bridge

At this spot over the Rancocas River, local Patriots destroyed a bridge to impede the British march across New Jersey after Clinton's evacuation of Philadelphia in June 1778. Clinton's secretary recorded the incident like this: "At a small distance from . . . [Mount Holly] a bridge was broken down by the rebels which, when our people were repairing, were fired upon by those villains from a house, two of which were taken prisoners, three killed and the other two ran into the cellar and fastened it so we were obliged to burn the house and consume them in it."

Mansfield

Petticoat Road Bridge Marker
Petticoat Road Bridge (1.25 miles south of Route 543)

Here, where the Petticoat Bridge spans Assiscunk Creek, is a historical marker that explains an attack by about four hundred American soldiers on a Hessian outpost on December 21, 1776. The Hessians retreated and reported to Col. Kurt von Donop that a large American force was gathering in Mount Holly.

It was all part of a plan to lure von Donop out of Bordentown and farther away from Trenton so he would not be in a position to aid the Hessians at Trenton during Washington's Christmas attack.

Von Donop took the bait and got his men out of Bordentown immediately to avoid being trapped on the river. He marched toward Mount Holly. As von Donop moved east, he was met by an American force of six hundred at the bridge, which lashed out a few volleys, then fell back to Mount Holly. If you continue south to the end of Petticoat Bridge Road and make a right on Jacksonville-Jobstown Road, you will see a small red brick building four-tenths of a mile up on the left. It was the Springfield Friends Meeting House. After the skirmishes at Petticoat Bridge, the Hessians used it as a hospital. A bloody Hessian handprint is said to be visible in the loft.

Medford

Adonijah Peacock Grave Site
Chairville Road (just before Route 70 intersection)

The cemetery at this spot was the family burial ground of the Peacock family. One family member, Adonijah, ran a one-man gunpowder mill nearby. While drying a batch of bad powder for the Continental army, Adonijah let it get too close to the fire. His tombstone tells the story.

Moorestown

The Smith-Cadbury Mansion
12 High Street
(609) 234-0330
HOURS: Tuesday, 1 P.M. to 3 P.M.

As the British moved from Philadelphia toward the Raritan Bay in June 1778, the huge British army (and its support personnel) invaded the Marlton–Moorestown–Mount Laurel area on June 19. It was a rainy night and soldiers and officers alike forced the locals into being hospitable. General von Knyphausen and other Hessian officers stayed here. Two legends arose out of the stay: one, that the Hessians plucked and cooked chickens in the family's parlor; and two, that Knyphausen had abominable table manners, choosing to eat with his hands rather than silverware. Run by the Historical Society of Moorestown, the house is filled with period furniture, including a chair that was a gift from Washington to a local Continental army officer.

Other Hessians stayed at what today is known as the Hessian House at Main and Schooley Avenues.

Moorestown Friends School and Meeting House
Chester Avenue and Main Street

The Hessians encamped in and around here on the night of June 19, 1778.

Mount Holly

Battle of Iron Works Hill Site
Pine Street (next to St. Andrew's Cemetery)

On December 23, 1776, Col. Samuel Griffin, in command of about six hundred American troops, dug in at this spot, awaiting the advance of Col. Kurt von Donop with a force of two thousand Hessians. After the Americans withdrew from Petticoat Bridge (see the Mansfield section of this chapter), they gathered here, while the Hessians took the high ground at the "The Mount" across the Rancocas River off Hillside Avenue (off Route 541). The Hessians shelled the town during the day, and Griffin fired back. At that point, von Donop believed a much larger American force occupied the Iron Works.

The volleys continued through December 23 and into Christmas Eve. Later that day, Griffin withdrew his men southeast toward Moorestown and the Hessians occupied Mount Holly without resistance.

There is a historical marker at the site which credits Griffin's decoy action with "reducing the enemy forces defending Trenton and assuring victory" for Washington. On a boulder surrounded by a group of large holly trees there is also a plaque applauding Griffin's "diversionary" tactic.

During their march across New Jersey in June 1778, the British destroyed the Iron Works as they passed through town.

The Friends Meeting House
77 Main Street

This Friends' establishment had barely opened (it was built in 1775) when the enemy commandeered the building over the objection of the pacifist Quakers and used it as a commissary.

The Old School
35 Brainerd Street
(609) 267-4337
HOURS: Wednesday, 1 P.M. to 4 P.M. May through October.

The Reverend John Brainerd, a staunch Patriot who preached independence from his church pulpit, also taught at this school. Perhaps that's why the British used the building, now the property of the National Society of Colonial Dames, as a stable for their horses during their evacuation of Philadelphia in June 1778. They also extracted some revenge by burning Brainerd's church down.

The Stephen Girard House
211 Mill Street
(Private)

This was the home of a wealthy foreign trader who named the ships in his fleet after his favorite philosophers. He contributed money to the American cause in both the Revolution and the War of 1812.

Mount Laurel

Thomas Smith House
General Clinton's Headquarters
1645 Hainesport–Mount Laurel Road
(Private)

Clinton got out the rain and stayed here on June 19, 1778, while marching his army out of Philadelphia on the way to the Raritan Bay. The force was intercepted by Washington outside Freehold, and the Battle of Monmouth ensued.

Evesham Friends Meeting House
Moorestown–Mount Laurel Road and Evesboro Road

While Clinton was cozy at the Thomas Smith House, his men huddled in and around this Quaker Meeting House. Clinton ordered them roused at 4 A.M. to continue their march.

Wharton State Forest

Batsto Village
Route 542 (ten miles west of Route 9 in New Gretna and eight
    miles east of Route 30 in Hammonton)
(609) 561-3262
HOURS: Park open year-round, 9 A.M. to 4 P.M.

Charles Read developed the bog iron industry in Burlington County and had forges at Aetna, Atsion, and Batsto. Unfortunately for Read, he had to either close or sell his shares of the furnaces before the war.

The furnace at Atsion Lake, also in Wharton State Forest off Route 206 just north of the Burlington County–Atlantic County border, was up and running during the war.

But it was Batsto, bought from Read by John Cox, that became the Continental army's leading supplier of cannons, munitions, tools, and other iron goods.

Today, Batsto is a restored village with thirty-three buildings reflecting the way it looked in the mid-1800s, when there was not only pig iron manufacturing but a glassworks as well.

Essex and Hudson Counties

These counties had a heavy concentration of English sympathizers, and their proximity to British-controlled New York made it very difficult for American Patriots to function.

The British held what today is Hudson County for most of the war. During the fall of New York in 1776, the Continental army abandoned the area and the British took over until the end. An argument can be made that Washington's retreat across New Jersey—which the history books say began after the fall of Fort Lee in November—actually began with the evacuation of the Hudson County area as early as September. It was then that Gen. Hugh Mercer's "flying camps" dismantled their forts and withdrew from the area.

Hudson County was the only place in New Jersey that never rebounded from the retreat, that never enjoyed a lasting American victory. The people there who wanted to reject British rule suffered as the Loyalists repeatedly pillaged their farms and homes.

In Essex, the Patriots had greater numbers, but eastern Essex held very little strategic importance with the British so close in Hudson. Remember, too, that in North Jersey, Elizabethtown was the commercial and cultural center. Newark was a smaller city and western Essex County was sparsely populated. In west Essex, Washington used the first ridge of the Watchung Mountains for spying on the British. That high rise also kept the British from making a run at the Americans at Morristown through Essex—they opted instead to try from Union and Middlesex Counties.

Bayonne (Hudson County)

Bergen Point Fort Site
Southernmost tip of Bayonne

Underneath the Bayonne Bridge, where the Kill Van Kull meets the Newark Bay, and on property now used by oil refineries, was the site of the Bergen Point Fort.

This fort was put on alert early in the war, when the British fleet sailed into New York in the summer of 1776. Americans feared the British would land at Bergen Point en masse and surround New York.

On July 18, a barge carrying redcoats landed at Bergen Point, but the Americans drove them back. On July 21, the Americans at the fort exchanged cannon fire with the British fleet. On August 26, shots were exchanged between Bergen Point and a British battery on Staten Island.

On August 30, Washington asked that the militia fortify this vulnerable spot as part of the "flying camps" under the direction of Gen. Hugh Mercer.

The point of the flying camps was to position soldiers around the New York City area in a number of spots from which they could be deployed quickly to wherever fighting broke out. There were about two thousand men in the flying camps. In New Jersey, some were at Bergen Point, Bergen Neck, Paulus Hook, and in the Perth Amboy area.

But as New York fell during the autumn of 1776, Mercer's flying camps disintegrated and the men at Bergen Point and Bergen Neck flew only to join Washington's retreat across New Jersey. By October 5, the Americans had evacuated the area, and the forts at Bergen Point and Bergen Neck had fallen into the hands of the jubilant Loyalists in the area.

The fort was the site of a number of small skirmishes throughout the war, as Patriots from Elizabethtown rowed over to harass or attempt to capture Loyalists.

Fort Delancey Site
West 52nd Street between Avenue B and Avenue C

A historical marker on Avenue B tells the story of this outpost, which was built by the Continental army in 1776 in what was then called Bergen Neck. Loyalists took over the fort in the fall of 1776 and held it until 1782.

A park seven blocks north of here is named after Gen. Hugh Mercer.

In 1780, the Loyalists abandoned Bergen Point and built a more substantial fort with a log fence at Bergen Neck. They named it Fort Delancey in honor of a prominent New York Tory. It became one of the blockhouses the British used specifically for woodcutting operations (see the North Bergen section of this chapter).

Belleville (Essex County)

Battle of Second River Sites

There is confusing information about battles near the junction of the Second River and the Passaic River on what today is the Newark-Belleville border.

Historic Roadsides in New Jersey (see the Research chapter) lists a battle here on September 27, 1778.

Battles and Skirmishes of the American Revolution, by David C. Munn (see the Research chapter), says two battles were fought here, one on January 27, 1777 (Munn writes, "Skirmish occurs between British foraging party and large body of rebels"), and one on June 1, 1779 ("Militia captures Tory named Lawrence"). *The WPA Guide to 1930s New Jersey* (see the Research chapter) says the Second River was "the scene of a rear guard action in 1777," without further explanation. Other accounts describe a conflict between the rear guard of Washington's retreating army and Gen. Charles Cornwallis's advancing redcoats after the fall of Fort Lee, but that would have been in late November 1776.

There are no markers for any battle near the junction of the Second and the Passaic where Main Street runs into Mill Street. The area today is overshadowed by a series of Route 21 overpasses and exit and entrance ramps.

One account of a battle at Second River has Americans on the west side of the Passaic River exchanging cannon fire with the British on the east (now Kearny). There was once a blue-and-white roadside marker on the Kearny side of the Passaic River on the Belleville Turnpike just east of the Passaic Avenue–River Road junction, but that is gone.

Belleville Reformed Church
171 Main Street
(973) 759-8152

At the corner of Belleville Street and Main Street is a stone Reformed Church that dates back to 1697. During the Revolution, the church (rebuilt in the 1720s and again in the nineteenth century) was passed by American troops on their retreat across New Jersey and British troops in pursuit.

According to legend, Americans used the bell tower at the church as a lookout and a sniper's nest. One of the snipers, Capt. Abraham Spear, is buried in the churchyard along with sixty-four other Revolutionary War veterans, including Henry Rutgers, for whom the state university is named.

East Orange (Essex County)

Watessing Skirmish Site
Vicinity of Main Street, North Munn Street, and Maple Avenue

During the British foraging attack of September 12–16, 1777 (see the Kearny section of this chapter), there was a running skirmish through this area as enemy soldiers rounded up all the livestock they could lay their hands on. New Jersey militia troops began to fire on the five hundred Hessians near what today is the Watessing section of Bloomfield and followed the enemy south. The outnumbered minutemen weren't able to slow the enemy cattle drive.

Jersey City (Hudson County)

Paulus Hook Fort Site
Intersection of Washington and Grand Streets

The red-white-and-blue park benches, street poles, garden fences, and garbage cans at the Paulus Hook Fort site belie the fact that the British held the fort for most of the war. In truth, the fort at Paulus Hook was a symbol of American failure.

In colonial times, Paulus Hook was a large spit of land jutting out into the Hudson, the closest point in New Jersey to New York City. It was the site of a ferry which brought travelers into Lower Manhattan. In the 1760s, Paulus Hook became a main transportation center, with twenty stagecoaches a day bringing people to the New York ferry.

Early in the war, Washington ordered two forts to be built on the hook. He saw the spit as a crucial location for defending the Hudson or launching an attack into New York.

By June 1776, Washington had set up his "flying camps"—a group of highly mobile attack units that were positioned around New York. Washington was expecting three or four thousand motivated men. He barely got two thousand—and not the quick-strike type of soldiers he had in mind. He put Gen. Hugh Mercer in charge of the flying camps.

On July 2, 1776, a few hundred men reported to Paulus Hook. In

Battle of Paulus Hook Monument

September, as the Continental army retreated through New York, the men at Paulus Hook began breaking the fort down. By the end of the month, they had abandoned it.

The British held the fort for the rest of the war. However, on August 19, 1779, Col. "Light-Horse" Harry Lee came over the marshes from Hackensack with four hundred men and attacked the fort in an early morning raid. The Americans overran the fort, took about one hundred fifty prisoners, and headed back to Hackensack.

The Apple Tree House
298 Academy Street
PHONE: Unavailable.
HOURS: Unavailable.

On President's Day in 1999, Richard Winant of the Paulus Hook section of Jersey City dressed as a redcoat corporal and marched in front of this house, saying, "Lord Cornwallis is pleased the rebels have yet to secure these premises and wants to see this building razed so as not to be reminded of past humiliation."

At this writing, the house is the property of the Provident Savings Bank of New Jersey, which planned to turn it into a drive-through branch when they purchased it in 1996. Local preservationists feel the house is in danger of falling into disrepair—the first step before demolition—and have asked the city to purchase it from the bank. The city is prepared to buy the house from the bank for $450,000 and to renovate it for some public use.

During the Revolution, the house was used by the Marquis de Lafayette while on a 1779 foraging expedition in Old Bergen. At that time, Washington visited here and dined with Lafayette under a backyard apple tree. (The tree was later toppled by a storm, and a walking stick made out of the wood was given to Lafayette in 1824 with an inscription describing the meeting.)

The house has other historical significance: it was once the home of the Van Wagenen family, which in 1650 received a deed for a substantial piece of Hudson County land from Peter Stuyvesant. Later, as the Quinn funeral home, it was the place where Mayor Frank Hague was served with a subpoena in 1954, after attending the wake of a former mayor, Frank Eggers.

Sip Manor Site
Corner of Newkirk Street and Bergen Avenue

This home was used by Cornwallis as a headquarters. It is said that he ordered the hanging of three suspected spies, who swung from the willow tree behind the house the next day.

In 1928, the house was moved to Westfield as the one of the center-pieces of the Wychwood development, one of the most exclusive neighborhoods in Union County, where it remains a private home today at 5 Cherry Lane.

Kearny (Hudson County)

Site of Clinton's Forage
West Bennett

On September 12, 1777, Gen. Henry Clinton sent two thousand British regulars, Hessians, and Tories through what today are Bergen, Essex, Hudson, and Union Counties in a four-pronged foraging attack to round up everything on four legs.

The four columns roamed the countryside, stealing livestock from American Loyalists as well as Patriots. On September 16, the elements of this horse, sheep, and cattle drive met up near the Schuyler estate, on high ground that today is the neighborhood of West Bennett Avenue and Bayard Street just east of River Bank Park. From there they headed south to Bergen Point, where the animals were loaded on barges and shipped across the Kill Van Kull to Staten Island.

Millburn (Essex County)

Washington Rock
End of Crest Drive
South Mountain Reservation

Overlooking the downtown areas of Millburn and Springfield to the southwest, this area is said to have been a lookout used by Washington in the weeks before the Battle of Springfield and during the battle itself, on June 23, 1780. Washington's main army was in Morristown at the time, and the British invaded Elizabethtown and Connecticut Farms and twice tried to advance to Morristown through Springfield (see the Union County chapter).

After being repulsed at Springfield the British "quit New Jersey soil forever," as the plaque on the rock here says.

The Hessian House
155 Millburn Avenue
(Private)

Legend has it that a pair of Hessians hid here during the Battle of Springfield.

Montclair (Essex County)

Old Crane Homestead
Corner of Valley Road and Claremont Avenue
(Private)

On this corner is a large boulder with a bronze plaque that says Washington stayed on this site on the night of October 26, 1780. Some accounts say Washington stayed two nights, the 26th and 27th. He was in this area visiting Lafayette, who was encamped with his troops further up Valley Road in what today is the business district of Upper Montclair.

The little city-owned memorial out in front of the existing house is famous in its own right: it was once listed in Ripley's *Believe It or Not* as "The World's Smallest Park."

The house where Washington stayed belonged to the Crane family, and another Crane house (Israel's, c. 1796) is the headquarters for the Montclair Historical Society. While the Israel Crane House obviously has no Revolutionary War significance, the historical society often puts on demonstrations of colonial living there, including Revolutionary War encampments. The Israel Crane house is at 110 Orange Road. Call (973) 744-1796.

Lafayette Site
Vicinity of 551 Valley Road

In this village-like neighborhood of Tudor storefronts is another little park. This one has a flagpole, a Daughters of the American Revolution plaque, and the stone doorstep of a long-gone house nearby, which Lafayette used as his headquarters. The park is the creation of Mr. Dominic Testa, a local optician, who bought the property from the nearby Commonwealth Club after a fire destroyed part of the club's building. Testa rescued the plaque and the stone doorstep from the Commonwealth Club and made a small monument park of his own.

"He's very patriotic," said his daughter, Mary Ellen Mercadante. "He's very American. You should see his eagle collection."

Newark (Essex County)

Military Park
Broad Street and Park Place

This is one of the oldest parks in America, laid out shortly after Robert Treat and a group from Connecticut relocated here in 1666 to build a theocracy.

During the Revolution, the park was known as the Lower Commons or the Lower Green. It was used as a parade ground for the militia, although it was literally in the shadow of an enemy church.

When Washington retreated across New Jersey in 1776, his troops camped here. One of the men was Thomas Paine, who is said to have written the opening lines of *The Crisis* while resting under a tree in Military Park.

In the park today is the Washington Plane Tree, a sycamore that was standing when Washington came through. At the south end of the park is the Liberty Pole, from which American colors flew in 1778 when the Continental army occupied the town.

(Note: It is worth the trip here to see Gutzon Borglum's bronze monument *The Wars of America.* Borglum is the artist who designed Mount Rushmore, and *The Wars of America* is one of his finest public works. The giant monument has forty-two figures in it, including a large group of Revolutionary War soldiers.)

Trinity Episcopal Cathedral
Broad Street and Park Place
(973) 624-4745

Trinity Church (now Trinity Cathedral), at the north end of Military Park, was the center for Loyalists in what was a politically divided Newark during the Revolution. The Reverend Dr. Isaac Browne was the minister there and one of leading Tories in North Jersey. As the war swung in the Patriots' favor, he fled to Canada where he eventually died, destitute.

During the war, the church was occupied by both armies, but suffered tremendously while in the hands of the Americans. The church was so badly damaged that the congregation applied for and received war reparations from Congress.

First Presbyterian Church
820 Broad Street
(973) 642-0260

Like Trinity, the First Presbyterian Church—"Old First"—was badly damaged in the war. Unlike Trinity, First Presbyterian was a center of Patriot activity. Like Trinity's Isaac Browne, the Reverend Alexander Macwhorter, Old First's minister, was driven from Newark. Unlike Browne, he was able to return.

The vocal Macwhorter retreated from Newark right after Washington's army in late 1776, knowing that the British would make life uncomfortable for him if he stayed. He returned after the British moved on and remained pastor of Old First until 1807.

Macwhorter's passion for the cause impressed Washington, and the two remained friends. In fact, Macwhorter sat in on several of Washington's councils of war.

Washington Park
Site of Newark Academy
Broad Street and Washington Place

Three blocks north of Military Park on Broad Street is Washington Park, known as the Upper Green in the early days. This was the site of the first Newark Academy (est. 1774), which was the target of a British attack on January 25, 1780. It seems the academy was doubling as a storage bin for American arms and a barracks, and the British burned the building during a surprise nighttime raid. A plaque on a boulder in the park tells the story.

Also in the park are a large bronze map of Washington's retreat across New Jersey, which passed through here, and a large J. Massey Rhind sculpture of Washington beside his steed on a man-made hill.

Plume House
407 Broad Street (at State Street)

In the shadow of New Jersey Transit's Broad Street station is the Plume House (c. 1710), which today is the rectory for the House of Prayer Episcopal Church.

During one of the enemy's many foraging parties, the lady of the house, Mistress Ann Van Wagenen, singlehandedly drove some Hessian pillagers from her property. Another time, she locked a Hessian in her icehouse.

Later in this house, the Reverend Hannibal Goodwin invented flexible photographic film, getting a patent for it in 1887.

Philips Park
Elwood Avenue and Elwood Place

In this small park was a monument marking the site of a Continental army encampment during Washington's retreat.

Lyons Farm School at Newark Museum
49 Washington Street
(973) 596-6550
HOURS: Open daily, noon to 5 P.M.

This schoolhouse was on Elizabeth Avenue at Chancellor (known as Pot Pie Lane) when the Continental army marched by in its retreat across New Jersey. Washington is said to have visited the school, which was later burned in a British raid. The brownstone that sits in the parking lot of the museum was built soon after to replace the original. It was moved to the museum site in 1938.

North Bergen (Hudson County)

Bull's Ferry Blockhouse Site
John F. Kennedy Boulevard and 74th Street

The British desperately needed firewood for the army and for the residences they maintained in New York, and the hard winter of 1779–80 wiped out their supply.

This area was densely wooded in Revolutionary War days, and the British decided to build a blockhouse here. They took out an ad in James Rivington's *New-York Gazetteer* for woodcutters and proceeded to build the fort. And a fort it was: three sides of the blockhouse were built against sheer rock. On the open side they built walls that offered three lines of defense. The first was a series of fallen trees with their exposed branches sharpened. The next was a log wall with portholes for cannons and muskets. If the Americans got through that, they would still have to cross a deep ditch to get to the enemy. The only entrance to the fort was a tunnel too narrow to allow men to come in two-by-two.

The fort was manned mostly by Loyalists, as soldiers and woodcutters. It was used not only for cutting and storing the precious commodity, but as a launch pad for foraging raids and other attacks.

These attacks forced the Continental army to support the Bergen militia's plan to shut down the fort. On July 21, 1780, Gen. "Mad" Anthony Wayne took a few hundred men and four heavy guns to a spot overlooking the fort and began shelling. After two hours, almost no damage had been done. Wayne saw British reinforcements coming across the Hudson and decided to retreat, but the men of Wayne's Pennsylvania Regiments charged the fort. They failed to penetrate the fort and fifteen were killed at the entrance, with another forty-six wounded.

The British abandoned and burned the fort two months later, opting to place their woodcutting operation at Fort Delancey.

Orange (Essex County)

First Presbyterian Church
Main Street and Scotland Road

There are a number of Revolutionary War soldiers and Patriots buried in the cemetery that surrounds the old stone church. In a prominent position in the cemetery is a weathered bronze statue honoring the "Dispatch Rider of the American Revolution." Dispatch riders provided the communications system of the war, carrying important messages from headquarters to command posts to the front lines.

But not all dispatch riders were put on pedestals. Washington wrote to Congress on December 1, 1776, that "I wish my letters of yesterday may arrive safe, being informed that the return express who had them was idling his time, and shewing [showing] them on the road."

Also, it was a dispatch rider who gave away the location of Gen. Charles Lee to British soldiers before they captured him at Basking Ridge (see the Somerset County chapter).

STEPHANIE DI IONNO

The Dispatch Rider, First Presbyterian Church, Orange

Tory Corner Marker, West Orange

Across the cemetery yard is a "Washington tree" planted in 1932 by the Daughters of the American Revolution to celebrate the two hundredth anniversary of Washington's birth. A plaque on a small wall tells the story. Nearby is the grave monument of another George Washington—this one is George Washington Smith, 1812–48.

West Orange (Essex County)

Eagle Rock Reservation

At approximately the site of the Highlawn Pavilion (elevation: 664 feet) was a lookout station used by Washington to spy on the British. The reservation is perched on the east side of the first ridge of the Watchung Mountains, and the view today is as remarkable as it was then.

Tory Corner Monument
Main and Washington Streets

Back in the old days, when most of Essex County was farmland, Nathaniel and Benjamin Williams had a large, profitable farm and a busy sawmill and gristmill around this site, which was called Williamstown. The Williams brothers were comfortable and saw no reason for a change of government. They were Loyalists, and other British-sympathizers often congregated on their property, which became known as Tory Corner.

Lower Delaware Region

CAMDEN, CUMBERLAND, GLOUCESTER, AND SALEM COUNTIES

Despite its proximity to Philadelphia, Camden County (then part of Gloucester) was relatively quiet during the war. The British marched through here after evacuating Philadelphia in June 1778, but there were very few encounters except a few around Haddonfield. Even so, the fact that the guns were quiet doesn't mean there wasn't any action. During 1777, the state lawmakers met in Haddonfield, where they formally rejected the status of colony, demanded loyalty from all citizens, and made it mandatory for all able-bodied men to join the militia.

Cumberland County was a Patriot hotbed, and the flames burned brightest in Bridgeton, the county seat. The town was home to the *Plain Dealer*, one of the colony's first radical newspapers; a proud liberty bell; Clarence Parvin, a Greenwich tea burner; Joseph Bloomfield, the tea burner's attorney and a Revolutionary War captain, who later became a general and served as governor; Dr. Jonathan Elmer, a Revolutionary War soldier and statesman; Col. David Potter; Maj. Almarin Brooks; Capt. Charles Glunn; Lt. Ebenezer Elmer, who later became a general; Joseph Jones, who served under Washington; Gen. James Giles; and a good number of enlisted men. Not bad, considering that at the time of the Revolution Bridgeton had about two hundred residents in total. If half were women, it's clear that the town's service rate was extraordinary. The homes of many of these men—most built after the war—are listed in *The Pictorial Guide to the Historic Buildings of Bridgeton*. This document is available at the county tourism office, which is in an old train station at the junction

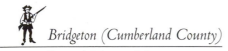

of Route 49 and Route 77. Call (609) 451-4802 or (609) 455-3230 ext. 262 for information.

Gloucester County was home to the two most important American Delaware River defenses—Fort Mercer at Red Bank (now a national park) and Fort Billings (in today's Paulsboro). The Battle of Red Bank was the largest battle in South Jersey.

In the fall of 1777, military activity at these two forts was increased in an effort to disrupt British supply ships headed upriver to Philadelphia. The British had taken the city, which at that time was the American capital, by invading overland on September 26. Now they wanted to clear the river to bring in more food, equipment, and troops.

The river forts proved to be more troublesome than the British anticipated, although by the end of the year the Americans had abandoned them under heavy enemy pressure.

Salem County was the site of a number of foraging expeditions early in 1778. Americans under Gen. "Mad" Anthony Wayne led a cattle drive out of the county, rounding up a hundred fifty head of Salem beef despite local farmers' best efforts to hide them. Wayne took the cattle to Valley Forge to feed the starving Continental army.

The British came a month later, with one thousand troops under Col. Charles Mawhood and five hundred Queen's Rangers under the notorious Maj. John Simcoe. These troops occupied Salem and engaged the local militia in bloody battles at Quinton's Bridge and the Hancock House.

The county did not suffer much else during the war, but it suffered afterwards because of the war. Before the war, Salem was the major river port along the Delaware, more popular than Philadelphia. But the war activity in and around Philadelphia proved the city's viability as a deepwater port, and Salem went into an economic decline.

Bridgeton (Cumberland County)

Potter's Tavern Museum
49–51 West Broad Street
(609) 451-4802
HOURS: Saturday, 11 A.M. to 3 P.M.; Sunday, noon to 4 P.M.

At a tavern on this spot a handwritten diatribe against British rule was posted on an outside wall every Thursday for all to see. The first one appeared on Christmas Day 1775, and locals claim it was New Jersey's first "newspaper."

The museum is a replica of the old tavern. The museum is one of five in Bridgeton, which boasts the largest historic district in New Jersey. (This may not be true, when you consider that all of Cape May is a national historic site. Nonetheless, Bridgeton's district takes in about one hundred commercial and residential blocks in the downtown area.) If you're up for something different, Bridgeton offers the Nail Mill Museum (with artifacts from the Industrial Revolution) and the George Woodruff Indian Museum (with over twenty thousand Lenni Lenape artifacts). Call the number above for information.

The Liberty Bell
Cumberland County Courthouse
Corner of Broad (Route 49) and Fayette Streets
(609) 451-8000
HOURS: Monday through Friday, 9 A.M. to 5 P.M.

On July 7, 1776, after Bridgeton residents got word from Philadelphia that the Declaration of Independence had been signed, this bell rang wildly throughout the day. It is displayed now at the courthouse, and a historical plaque tells the story.

Camden (Camden County)

Site of Cooper's Ferry
Cooper Avenue and Second Street

Near the public library is a faded blue-and-white historical sign that marks the spot of Cooper's Ferry, which connected the town of the same name (later called Camden) to Philadelphia. During the British occupation of Philadelphia, there were a number of skirmishes in this area, including the New Jersey militia's capture of twenty British sailors on December 15, 1777.

Site of Foraging Skirmish
709 Market Street

On March 2, 1778, as Gen. Anthony Wayne and his men headed back toward Valley Forge with a hundred fifty head of Salem cattle for the starving men there (see the introduction to this chapter), he encountered British resistance near this spot. With support from troops under Count Casimir Pulaski, Wayne was able to keep the herd intact.

Elmer (Salem County)

Ye Olde Centerton Inn

(609) 358-3201
Intersection of Routes 540 and 553

Built in 1706, the inn was a stagecoach stop and tavern during the war, and it operates as restaurant today. It is the oldest continuously operating inn in New Jersey and the second oldest in the country.

Gen. Anthony Wayne and his staff held a number of strategy sessions here in conjunction with the foraging missions in Salem County. Lafayette also had occasion to stop here.

"We're the best-kept historical secret in New Jersey," said Cosmo Terrigno Jr., who owns the inn with his father.

Elsinboro (Salem County)

Holmeland

410 Fort Elfsborg–Hancock's Bridge Road
(Private)

This was the home of Col. Benjamin Holme of the South Jersey militia, who fought at Quinton's Bridge. On March 24, 1778, six days after the battle at Quinton's Bridge, British Col. Charles Mawhood led a raid on Holme's property. The British stole everything they could carry, then set fire to the main house, outbuildings, and barns.

One of Holme's prized possessions was an eight-foot Thomas Wagstaffe Chippendale clock, which chimed six different tunes. That clock ended up at Gen. William Howe's headquarters in New York, and a Salem woman, Ester Gibbon, noticed the unique clock during a visit to the city. After the war, this same Ester Gibbon married Holme and told him about the clock. Holme went to New York and reclaimed it. The clock today is at the Salem County Historical Museum in the Alexander Grant House at 79–83 Market Street in Salem (609) 935-5004.

Greenwich (Cumberland County)

The Greenwich Tea Party Monument

Corner of Ye Greate Street and Market Lane

On December 22, 1774—a year after the Boston Tea Party—a group of twenty-three Cumberland County men conspired to have a little tea party of their own.

The planning began when the British brig *Greyhound* came up the Delaware Bay, destined for Philadelphia with a cargo of heavily taxed English tea. The captain had heard that there might be trouble in Philadelphia—a shipload of English tea had been turned away just weeks earlier and the captain feared a tea burning might be awaiting him there.

He took the *Greyhound* up the Cohansey River into Greenwich, and the tea was unloaded and stored at the home of Loyalist Daniel Bowen. Word spread, and a committee of Cumberland County Patriots was formed to discuss how to deal with the matter. But while they were talking, a group of more militant young men decided to take matters into their own hands.

The group included eight sets of brothers—the Elmers, the Ewings, the Fithians, the Howells, the Hunters, the Newcombs, the Piersons, and the Seelys.

Most of them met at the Howell house in Shiloh and rode to Greenwich, where they picked up the Fithians. Dressed—they might say disguised—as Indians, they broke into Bowen's home and carried the tea to Market Square, where the monument stands today. There they started a bonfire and celebrated as the rest of the villagers gathered round.

The tea owners demanded justice and asked Sheriff Jonathan Elmer to bring the suspects to trial. He did just that. But since two of his brothers—Ebenezer and Timothy—were in the "Indian" war party, the sheriff also made sure he picked a jury of friends, relatives, and political confederates. Despite numerous witnesses and other overwhelming evidence, the tea burners were acquitted.

New Jersey's royal governor, William Franklin, was furious. Although he was the son of Benjamin Franklin, William Franklin was staunchly behind the British and ordered a second trial. He appointed fellow British-sympathizer Bowen—the man from whom the tea had been stolen—to prosecute the tea burners a second time. Bowen tried to rig the process as Elmer had, but couldn't find a jury that shared his sympathies. The men were acquitted again.

Many of the tea burners went on to great things. Almost all served in the Continental army or the New Jersey militia.

Richard Howell became governor of New Jersey in 1793. (Joseph Bloomfield, the attorney who defended the men, was governor from 1801 to 1812.) Ebenezer Elmer became a U.S. congressman, and Timothy Elmer and Joel Fithian were members of the New Jersey Legislature. Andrew Hunter Jr. became the head chaplain of the U.S. Navy and Philip Vickers Fithian served as chaplain for the New Jersey militia.

This monument is an eight-foot granite structure with a bronze plaque depicting the men, disguised as Indians, burning the tea. Another plaque lists the names of all twenty-three tea burners.

Each year around December 22 a cannon-firing ceremony is held at the monument.

The Philip Vickers Fithian House
Tea Burner Lane

Before the tea burning, the burners met at the home of Philip Vickers Fithian, who later became chaplain for the New Jersey militia. He died at Fort Washington.

The Fithian house is a red clapboard house at the end of this road.

It is unclear whether Fithian died of battle injury or illness, but a diary entry three months before he died gives a clue:

"In every Apartment are many in the Dysentary. Many have putrid fevers; Yet to such places, must our Youth do & mix with such Diseases; & here I must daily visit among many in contagious Disorder. . . . But I am not discouraged, nor dispirited; I am willing to hazard & suffer equally with my Countrymen since I have a firm conviction that I am in my duty."

The Gibbon House
Ye Greate Street
(609) 455-4055
HOURS: Daily, noon to 4 P.M. except Mondays; Sunday, 2 P.M.
         to 5 P.M. The house closes for the winter from around
         Christmas until April 1.

This house is the headquarters of the Cumberland County Historical Society. Inside are a number of Revolutionary War artifacts including the sword of David Potter, a colonel in the Cumberland County militia. Potter's descendants have served in nearly every U.S. war or conflict up until World War I, and their individual sabers are displayed.

Haddonfield (Camden County)

Indian King Tavern Museum
233 Kings Highway
(609) 429-6792
HOURS: Wednesday through Saturday, 10 A.M. to noon, 1 P.M.
         to 4 P.M.; Sunday, 1 P.M. to 4 P.M. Closed on Wednesdays
         following major holidays.

MARK DI IONNO

Haddonfield's Indian King Tavern

The New Jersey Legislature met three times in this building throughout 1777: from January 29 to March 18, from May 7 to June 7, and from September 3 to September 24.

The first of these sessions was held about a month after the Battles of Trenton and Princeton, which renewed the Patriots' urgent desire for independence.

A list of the legislative acts illustrates that urgency:

— March 15, the first state militia act is passed, requiring all males from ages sixteen to fifty to drill once a month in local regiments. Fines can be imposed for absenteeism.

— May 10, Governor William Livingston unveils the state seal. New Jersey officially rejects the status of British colony.

— June 4, a law establishes new election procedures. Citizens are required to pledge allegiance to the new nation before being allowed to vote.

— June 5, general amnesty is provided to all Loyalists, Tories, and sympathizers to the Crown so that they may take an oath of allegiance to the new nation. Those who do not take the oath by August 1 will have their property seized.

→ September 20, the death penalty now applies to treason.

→ September 20, certain goods such as "pitch [a tarlike substance], tar, turpentine or naval stores [shipping equipment] are to be sold exclusively to the military or they will be confiscated. Export of such items is forbidden."

The British also used the tavern during their march through New Jersey in June 1778 after evacuating Philadelphia.

The tavern has been restored to look exactly as it did in Revolutionary War times.

Across the street from the Indian King, at 258 Kings Highway, is the Old Guardhouse. An underground tunnel led from the Indian King, where Loyalists were tried by the state Council of Safety, to the guardhouse. The old jail today is a commercial building.

Down the street from both buildings at the intersection of Kings Highway and Haddon Avenue are a pair of buttonwood trees on which hang signs explaining the origins of the road in 1681 and marking the spot where the British army marched.

Lower Alloways Creek Township (Salem County)

The Hancock House
Salem–Hancock's Bridge Road
(609) 935-3218
HOURS: Unavailable.

In the early morning of March 21, 1778, Maj. John Simcoe and his three hundred Queen's Rangers surrounded a house owned by Judge William Hancock, where thirty Salem militiamen were sleeping. Two sentries were bayoneted, and Simcoe's Rangers rushed the house. Accounts vary: some say all thirty Americans were killed, others say twenty. One thing is certain: the outnumbered militiamen didn't have a chance against Simcoe's Raiders, a group of combat-hardened Tories who carried out similar guerrilla missions in New York, Pennsylvania, and elsewhere in New Jersey (see the Somerset County chapter). Most of the people killed were middle-aged men or teenaged boys. One of the fatalities was Hancock himself—ironic, because he was an influential Loyalist in the region. He had been driven out of his house, but he had returned just that night.

Simcoe was in Salem as part of the British foraging mission in March 1778. Before the massacre at Hancock's Bridge, as it is often called, Simcoe was with Col. Charles Mawhood in the attack at Quinton's Bridge on March 18. Simcoe was reportedly angry that they couldn't do more bodily harm to the militia during that skirmish, and asked Mawhood to let him go after the militia's stronghold in the village at Hancock's Bridge. Simcoe's men arrived that night in boats on the Alloways Creek during a heavy rain, looking forward to a surprise attack and a battle with a much larger force. Simcoe also sent in a detachment on foot, and another to block potential escape routes. It was a lot of troop movement for a little battle, though. Most of the Salem militia had dispersed, leaving only the men at the judge's house.

It is said that the house has bloodstains in the attic from the attack and that ghosts sometimes reenact the brutal encounter. Maybe. But historical significance and spooky stuff aside, the house also has important architectural value. It is an outstanding example of the Flemish masonry that is so prevalent in this region. There are patterned brick designs on the back and front walls and a zigzag effect on the side walls. The initials W-H-S for William Hancock and his wife, Sarah, and the date they built the house, 1734, are spelled out in brick and stacked in a pyramid under the roof apex.

The Hancock House is connected with Fort Mott State Park, and the telephone number is for the park office. At this writing, funds are being raised to reopen the house to the public.

National Park (Gloucester County)

Fort Mercer Site
Red Bank Battlefield
James and Ann Whithall House
End of Hessian Road
(609) 853-5120
HOURS: Outdoor sites open every day, dawn to dusk;
     Whithall House Museum open Wednesday through Friday,
     9 A.M. to noon and 1 P.M. to 4 P.M.

The Battle of Red Bank occurred on October 22, 1777, when a force of twelve hundred Hessians under Col. Kurt von Donop attacked about four hundred men under Col. Christopher Greene.

Von Donop marched down from Burlington County and spent the night in Haddonfield. He arrived at Fort Mercer at noon, showing his superior

Memorial Wall, Red Bank Battlefield

force, and sent an emissary to the fort with surrender terms. When the terms were denied, von Donop arranged an attack. What the Hessian leader did not know was that the fort had been refortified and that an existing exterior embankment was now a dummy wall. As his men made their way to the real wall, Greene was waiting. When the Hessians got within musket range, Greene ordered his men to fire. What happened next was carnage unparalleled in other New Jersey battles. About four hundred Hessians were killed in the forty-minute battle, including von Donop, who had a musket ball rip through his leg. Another one hundred were wounded and captured. The American deaths numbered fourteen, with another twenty-three wounded.

Not only were the Hessians assaulted from land, but American boats on the Delaware sent in some fire.

Legend has it that Ann Whithall refused to leave the house during the battle, choosing instead to work on her spinning wheel. When a cannonball struck the wall near where she was working, she picked up her wheel and yarn and continued working in the basement.

After the battle, the house was used as a hospital, and Ann Whithall helped care for the injured. The Quaker woman is said to have scolded the mercenary Hessians for coming to the colonies to fight.

The American victory was impressive, but it did not prove to be militarily significant in the defense of the Delaware. About three weeks later,

MARK DI IONNO

The Whithall House, Red Bank Battlefield

Gen. Charles Cornwallis and two thousand men drove the Americans from Fort Mifflin, across the river in Pennsylvania. The retreating troops gathered at Fort Mercer, but when Cornwallis began coming across the river, Greene evacuated the fort, burning everything the British might find useful.

However, the battle may have had even greater significance. The American win at Red Bank, coupled with the British surrender at Saratoga five days earlier, helped persuade the French to enter the war. Clearly, the French saw that the cause was not lost.

There is an eighty-foot monument at the forty-four-acre park, along with a commemorative wall with bronze depictions of the battle. The park has a beautiful view of the river and its bridges: you can see container ships silently negotiating the Delaware and airplanes coming in to land at Philadelphia International Airport.

The Whithall House Museum has artifacts from the battle, including musket balls, cannonballs, belt buckles, and eating utensils. An exhibit explains the battle to control the Delaware. Another explains the use of the chevaux-de-frise. These were large subsurface boxes filled with rocks that had long spiked poles protruding from them at forty-five-degree angles. The spikes were aimed at ships coming upriver, to either stop them or puncture their hulls.

Paulsboro (Gloucester County)

Fort Billings Site
Beacon Avenue, between Fifth and Sixth Streets
(856) 423-5698

Fort Mercer has monuments and a museum, Fort Billings has a tin sign and oil refinery tanks. This may be the most forgotten significant Revolutionary War site in New Jersey.

Fort Billings was the nation's first federal government installation. On July 5, 1776—the day after the signing of the Declaration of Independence—the new federal lawmakers purchased land where Mantua Creek empties into the Delaware.

Fort Billings was also the first defensive position designed by Gen. Thaddeus Kosciusko, who helped design the other Delaware forts and devised American defensive strategies at Saratoga and West Point.

Kosciusko's fortification was inspected by Washington himself, accompanied by the Marquis de Lafayette, on August 1, 1777. He visited Red Bank the same day.

By October 3, Fort Billings was no more. The British broke through the chevaux-de-frise below the fort and landed five hundred men on the shore. The one hundred fifty Americans abandoned the fort, burning most of it as they fled.

MARK DI IONNO

Fort Billings Site, Paulsboro

As you enter Paulsboro—a gritty industrial town most famous for its outstanding high school wrestling and football teams—signs tell you the town is "the home of Fort Billings." Some signs even have a Continental army soldier on them. The site, however, isn't that easy to find. There are no signs and no one seems to know where it is. Common sense tells you it is west of downtown, toward the river. Take Billingsport Road to North Delaware Street and make a left. At the end of North Delaware is Fort Billings Park, a narrow strip of land sandwiched between two oil refineries. The actual site of the fort is on land owned by the GATX oil refinery, but two monuments near the fence mark the approximate spot.

Penns Grove (Salem County)

Helms Cove Tavern
21 East Maple Avenue
(Private)

This house was hit by a cannonball from the British frigate *Roebuck* on March 7 or 8, 1776. A few days earlier the American brig *Lexington* had encountered the *Roebuck* and the *Liverpool* off the coast of Salem. Other ships, too, harassed the British as they tried to control the Delaware River. Onlookers from the shore taunted the British, and the captain of the *Roebuck* fired his guns landward.

Quinton (Salem County)

Quinton's Bridge Battle Site
Route 49

Three days before the massacre at Hancock's Bridge, the Patriots were dealt a beating at Quinton's Bridge. As with the Hancock incident, historical accounts of the battle at Quinton's Bridge widely vary. Some accounts put the death toll at seven, others as high as thirty to forty.

The fight occurred on March 18, 1778. Three hundred Salem and Cumberland County militia were stationed in defensive positions on the south side of Alloways Creek. The enemy—led by Mawhood and Simcoe—took up positions on the other side. On the night of March 17, Mawhood moved groups of men into concealed positions. The next morning he withdrew the rest of his men back toward Salem. The Americans gave chase—right into the British trap. They were soon surrounded on three sides as

Mawhood's troops wheeled around. The casualty number, be it seven or forty, was surprisingly low for such an overwhelming rout.

Today, the bridge over Alloways Creek on Route 49 is easy to miss. The creek is little more than a stream, and the bridge—which is very close to where the original was—is on the same plane as the rest of the road. A historic plaque marks the spot. Another landmark of the battle is Smick's Hardware and Lumber, on the north side of the bridge.

 *Salem (Salem County)*

St. John's Episcopal Church
Corner Market and Grant Streets

This church was built in 1728 and badly damaged during the British foraging raid in March 1778.

Salem Friends Meeting
East Broadway
(609) 935-3381

British soldiers camped in and around here during their occupation of Salem. After the war, trials of local Tories were held here. Many had their property confiscated.

Stow Creek Township (Cumberland County)

The Howell House
172 Shiloh Road

The tea burners met here at the home of the Howell brothers before riding into Greenwich to Philip Vickers Fithian's house.

The front of this farmhouse remains similar to the original and is being restored by the current owner.

Woodbury (Gloucester County)

Woodbury Friends Meeting
124 North Broadway
(609) 845-5080

This Quaker Meeting House, built in 1716, was used as a hospital during the war.

The John Cooper House
Across from Gloucester County Courthouse
North Broad Street
(Private)

This large red brick home belonged to John Cooper, whose sister was Ann (Cooper) Whithall. When Cornwallis's five thousand troops occupied the area following the evacuation of Fort Mercer, the British general made this home his headquarters.

The Hunter-Lawrence-Jessup House
58 North Broad Street
(609) 845-7881
HOURS: First and third Monday of each month and every
Wednesday and Friday, 1 P.M. to 4 P.M.

This house is headquarters of the Gloucester County Historical Society. During the Revolution, it was owned by Andrew Hunter, a Greenwich tea burner.

Mercer County

Named for Gen. Hugh Mercer, who was killed in the Battle of Princeton, the county was the scene of the ten crucial days that many historians think changed the course of the war.

Many historians consider the Battle of Trenton, specifically, the turning point of the war, largely because it was a major morale-building win just five weeks after Washington was forced to abandon the Hudson and retreat across New Jersey.

After losing men and supplies at Fort Washington and Fort Lee (see the Bergen County chapter), Washington did all he could to keep his army together. But as he marched through Newark, New Brunswick, and Trenton, Washington got increasingly bad reports about the shrinking numbers of Continental army volunteers and available New Jersey militia. It seemed that the colonists were more anti-British when the British weren't here. Once the British regulars and Hessians invaded the state and had Washington on the run, sentiment favoring the cause shifted to general apathy.

Nowhere is this documented better than in William M. Dwyer's book *The Day Is Ours! An Inside View of the Battles of Trenton and Princeton* (see the Research chapter). Dwyer uses letters from soldiers and regular people to tell the story of desertion and dismay in these days, which were described by Thomas Paine as "the times that try men's souls."

During this period the British were sharply divided on how to end the war. The British commander in chief, Gen. William Howe, wanted a political solution. He had the support of the Loyalists and Tories, who equaled the rebels in number. Now, hoping to gather the support of those who were undecided, he offered a variety of amnesty and allegiance-swearing programs that were supposed to protect the locals against the invading army.

On the other hand Gen. Charles Cornwallis, staying on Washington's heels throughout Bergen County, Newark, and New Brunswick, wanted to finish Washington off and was frustrated by Howe's lack of aggression. Many in the British command agreed with Cornwallis: the war was won, why prolong it? Hit Washington hard, send his rookie soldiers back to their farms, and sail home. Instead, Howe made plans for winter encampments.

Washington crossed the Delaware into Pennsylvania on December 7, 1776, taking all available boats with him to the other side. As he set up camp directly across from McKonkey's Ferry, he knew three things. First, his force of six thousand men would be cut to fourteen hundred when enlistments expired on December 31. Second, if the Delaware froze in midwinter and Howe could be convinced to go on the attack, the British could march across the river and stamp him out. Third, Congress and the people of the colony desperately wanted to see a victory—any victory—to boost confidence in him and the cause.

He decided Trenton was the place to get that win.

That is how the stage was set for Mercer County's major role in the war—the battles at Trenton and Princeton, and Washington's escape to Morristown.

Hamilton

John Abbott II House
2200 Kuser Road
(609) 585-1686
HOURS: Saturday and Sunday, noon to 5 P.M.

During the British occupation of Trenton, Gen. William Howe wanted to confiscate all of colonial New Jersey's printed money. The state treasurer, Samuel Tucker, hid the money in barrels and other containers in the cellar of this house. A barmaid named Mary Pointing overheard the plan and told Howe. A group of British soldiers went out to the house, overwhelmed the guards, and took the loot to Howe.

Hopewell Boro

The John Hart House
60 Hart Road
(Private)

John Hart was an elder statesmen of the Revolutionary cause, nearly sixty-five years old when the fighting began. A successful farmer, he had been a force in New Jersey politics for fifteen years before the Revolution. One of the most influential men on the side of independence, he served in the Provincial Congress and the Continental Congress and was a signer of the Declaration of Independence. An outspoken enemy of the king, he was harassed often by the British. His farm and mills were destroyed, and he had to abandon his home a number of times to avoid arrest. The Continental army camped on Hart's farm and two adjacent properties on June 23, 1778, on their way to the Battle of Monmouth.

Hart is buried at the Old Baptist School Church Cemetery on West Broad Street. The church and the school across the street at 19 West Broad Street doubled as hospitals in the Revolution.

Hopewell Township

The Hunt House
595 Province Line Road
(Private)

Here Washington held his celebrated council of war before the Battle of Monmouth. Some historians say it was the greatest single assemblage of American officers in the war. With Washington were Nathaniel Greene, Charles Lee, Anthony Wayne, the Marquis de Lafayette, and Alexander Hamilton, to name a few. Many agreed with Lee that as the Americans followed the British, who were on their way to Sandy Hook (see the Monmouth and Burlington County chapters), they should approach the British timidly. Washington won out, but put the reluctant Lee in charge of the advance force, a tactical error that almost cost the Americans the battle.

Washington Crossing State Park
355 Washington Crossing–Pennington Road (Route 546)
(609) 737-0623
HOURS: Outdoor areas open every day, dawn till dusk.

Washington Crossing State Park is an eight-hundred-acre retreat eight miles north of Trenton on Route 29, which runs along the Delaware River. It was the site of the Johnson and McKonkey ferries, which were less used than the ones at Coryell's Ferry (now Lambertville).

Washington planned to take Trenton in the early morning of December 26, correctly assuming that the Hessians would be hung over from

MARK DI IONNO

The Ferry House, Washington Crossing State Park

holiday festivities. The Hessian commander, Col. Johann Rall, had a reputation as a drunkard and Washington guessed that he would be unprepared
for an attack.

Washington ordered Gen. John Cadwalader to attack the Hessians at
Bordentown so they could not reinforce the Trenton Hessians (see the Bordentown and Mount Holly sections of the Burlington County chapter). He
also counted on Gen. James Ewing to bring one thousand men in south of
Trenton at Assunpink Creek. Both failed to cross the Delaware because of
the severity of the winter storm. (It should be noted that the river is wider
in those spots.)

Washington's men gathered on the Pennsylvania side of the Delaware on Christmas night, 1776. It took nine hours in an intensifying rain,
sleet, and snow storm to get the twenty-four hundred men across the ice-
chunked river to the Jersey side. They landed on the banks north of the bridge
near the Nelson House and took two routes to Trenton.

(Note: There is a separate Washington Crossing Park on the Pennsylvania side of the river. It also has much to offer. Call [215] 493-4076 for
information.)

The Nelson House

(609) 737-1783
HOURS: Limited access in summer months only.

This is the remaining part of a ferry house that the Americans used after they landed. It is alongside the river on the extreme southwest corner of the park property, but it is maintained and operated by the Washington Crossing Association of New Jersey. The crossing is reenacted near here each Christmas Day. Call the main park number (609) 737-0623 for details.

The Johnson Ferry House

(609) 737-2515
HOURS: Wednesday through Sunday, 9 A.M. to 4:30 P.M.

This house was owned by Rut Johnson, who was licensed to take travelers from New Jersey to Pennsylvania. (McKonkey's Ferry operated in the opposite direction.) Washington and his staff came to this house after disembarking and finalized plans for the attack. They waited here for hours while all the troops and equipment arrived. The interior of the house is done in period furniture to replicate an eighteenth-century ferry master's house.

The Visitors' Center and Museum

(609) 737-9303
HOURS: Wednesday through Sunday, 9 A.M. to 4:30 P.M.

At the visitors' center you can meet a living Revolutionary War "legend" in Harry Kels Swan, who probably has the world's largest private collection of Revolutionary War artifacts. More than nine hundred items from the Swan Foundation Collection are displayed in the museum here.

The Swan Collection was started in 1795 by Swan's great-great-grandfather Samuel Swan, a Somerset County doctor and New Jersey congressman who was born in 1776.

"Dr. Samuel was the first; he began by saving medical equipment," Swan said. "His son Jacob added considerably to the collection and his son, also Jacob, contributed a wealth of books and prints. My father, Peter, was an avid collector up until his death in 1975."

At this writing, Swan is working full-time at the visitors' center and loves to talk about his collection, especially how it relates to education.

"It's rare to find a place where you can bring in kids to see the actual artifacts carried by the boys in the Revolution," he said. "Here they can actually handle some of the artifacts—a powder horn, a flintlock pistol, America's first dollar bill."

The prized possession here is the scarlet uniform coat of Col. Johann Rall, the Hessian commander who died at the Battle of Trenton. As he lay dying, Rall asked that the uniform coat be given to Washington.

The museum has another artifact that passed through Washington's hands: the bronze medal awarded to him by Congress for forcing the British to evacuate Boston in March 1776. Also in the collection is a silver medal given John Paul Jones for his naval victory with the *Bonhomme Richard* over the HMS *Serapis* off the coast of Scotland on September 23, 1779.

The Bear Tavern
Intersection of Washington Crossing–Pennington Road
    (Route 546) and Trenton-Harbourton Road (Route 579)
(609) 737-0623
HOURS: Monday through Friday, 9 A.M. to 5 P.M.

This building today is the park headquarters and information center. At the time of the crossing, it was a tavern. Washington and his officers met there briefly before embarking on the march to Trenton. Gen. Nathaniel Greene took his column down what today is Route 31 into the heart of Trenton. Gen. John Sullivan went down roads that are today Grand Avenue and Sullivan's Way. There seems to be some disagreement as to exactly where the army split up. Some historians say they split at the Bear Tavern.

But in the small Historic Crossroads Park at the intersection of Upper Ferry Road (Route 634) and Grand Avenue (Route 579) in Ewing Township is a plaque asserting that Greene and Sullivan parted there.

Lawrenceville

Shabbaconk Creek
Route 206 just south of Notre Dame High School

At this stream in what was then called Maidenhead, Col. Edward Hand and a large force of Americans intercepted Cornwallis's army as it marched to Trenton on January 2, 1777. Washington had deployed this force for a delaying action—to fight the enemy long enough to allow Washington and the main army to dig in at Assunpink Creek. Hand engaged the British until Cornwallis ordered his men to bring up the artillery to blast past the pesky rebels. But before Cornwallis could get the big guns lined up, Hand withdrew.

This is another engagement whose exact history is unclear. Some say it actually occurred at Five Mile Run, a larger stream up the road just south of the present Rider University. Also, there may have been two or more engagements. Part of the strategy of a delaying action is to make an enemy stop to fight as much as possible. Col. Mark Boatner, in *Landmarks of the American Revolution* (see the Research chapter), writes that Hand "ordered a slow retreat as superior enemy forces moved south from Lawrence. . . . Wherever a good delaying position could be organized, Hand halted his troops for a stand."

Boatner is right. It took Cornwallis eight hours to march the final eight miles into Trenton. He arrived in the late afternoon, too late to engage Washington in a lengthy battle (see the Assunpink Creek Battle entry in the Trenton section of this chapter).

Lawrenceville Presbyterian Church
2688 Main Street
(609) 896-1212

John Hart belonged to the congregation of this church, which was known as the Maidenhead Presbyterian Church at the time of the Revolution. Another member was Elias Philips, the scout who led Washington's army from Trenton to Princeton. Philips is buried here.

Princeton

Princeton Battlefield State Park
500 Mercer Street
(609) 921-0074

Early on January 3, while Cornwallis dreamed about a glorious morning attack on the weary Americans holed up on the south side of the Assunpink Creek, Washington and his army began to move out. Cornwallis had told his officers, "We'll bag the fox in the morning," after the British made three unsuccessful runs at the bridge over the creek.

But the fox—Gen. George Washington—had other ideas. Washington's chief strategy was simple: keep the army intact. Do not incur heavy losses in casualties or captures but hit the British rear guard at Princeton before escaping to the Watchungs. So while the British slept, Washington slipped away. Wrapping the horses' feet in cloth to muffle the sound of their hooves, the army pulled out in the middle of the night, leaving behind a few men to stoke the campfires to make the British think the army was still in camp.

The Americans reached Princeton just before dawn.

The battle began when Gen. Hugh Mercer's force of about three hundred fifty men encountered two British regiments and a unit of mounted troops under Lt. Col. Charles Mawhood. Mercer positioned himself between Mawhood and the main American army, and the fighting began in Thomas Clarke's orchard. What followed was eighteenth-century warfare at its bloodiest. The British charged through volleys of American fire and bayoneted the outnumbered Americans. Mercer, determined not to surrender, tried to rally his men around him but was stabbed seven times. He was carried to Clarke's house, where he died an excruciating death nine days later.

Here Washington again added to his legend. As Mercer's men retreated in disorder, Washington rode to the front with the rest of the army and, exposing himself to two volleys of enemy fire, got the men to regroup. The British, now seeing they were outnumbered, retreated in the face of American guns. The Americans then advanced into Princeton, driving the remaining British from Nassau Hall and the rest of town.

The fifty-acre battlefield park is split down the middle by Mercer Road. On the east side of the road is the three-hundred-year-old "Mercer Oak," the tree near which Mercer was bayoneted. Across the street is the four-columned battle memorial. A plaque behind the memorial says, "Near here lie buried the American and British officers and soldiers who fell in the Battle of Princeton, January 3rd, 1777."

The Princeton Battlefield Memorial

MARK DI IONNO

MARK DI IONNO

Memorial Plaque, Princeton Battlefield

The Thomas Clarke House

(609) 921-0074

HOURS: Wednesday through Saturday, 9 A.M. to noon, 1 P.M.
to 4:30 P.M.; Sunday, 1 P.M. to 4:30 P.M.

Thomas Clarke was a Quaker farmer living peacefully on two hundred acres
on the outskirts of Princeton village when history happened in his orchard
and fields. After the battle, his house was used as a hospital for American and British wounded. Gen. Hugh Mercer was cared for there by Dr.
Benjamin Rush, a Continental army surgeon from Philadelphia who had
signed the Declaration of Independence. (A year after the battle, Rush wrote
an anonymous letter to Patrick Henry suggesting Washington be replaced.
Henry forwarded the letter to Washington, who recognized Rush's penman-
ship and confronted him. Rush resigned.)

The house serves as the Princeton Battlefield State Park museum, and
the historian there is John Mills, one of New Jersey's most knowledgeable

people in Revolutionary War matters. The house is filled with weaponry of the war and furniture of the period. Mills himself is worth the trip, dressed always in soldier's garb and ready to answer any questions about the ten crucial days.

Nassau Hall
Princeton University at Nassau Street
(609) 258-3603
TOURS AVAILABLE: Monday through Saturday, 10 A.M., 11 A.M., 1:30 P.M., and 3:30 P.M.; Sunday, 1:30 P.M. and 3:30 P.M.

Nassau Hall, built in 1754, was the main building on the Princeton campus. During the war both armies used it frequently as a barracks and a hospital, leaving it in shambles. The British held it during the Battle of Princeton until American artillery under the direction of Alexander Hamilton arrived. Two cannonballs hit the building, and one of them crashed through the brick walls and landed in the main hall where the soldiers were gathered. They promptly surrendered. There is an enduring story that the shot tore through a portrait of King George II and that the British took this as a bad omen. The frame of that portrait still hangs in the main room, now holding a portrait of Washington by Charles Willson Peale.

The building was vacant and in disrepair when mutineers of the Pennsylvania Line occupied it in 1781 on their way to confront Congress in Philadelphia. Here Gen. "Mad" Anthony Wayne negotiated an end to the situation.

From June 24 to November 3, 1783, Congress convened here, driven out of Philadelphia not by the British but by about three hundred disgruntled Continental army veterans in search of back pay. During this session Congress officially thanked Washington for his service to the country. It was also here that Congress received word that the Treaty of Paris had been signed, officially ending the war.

Maclean House
Princeton University at Nassau Street
(609) 258-3603

The house is located to the right of the main gates of the university off Nassau Street. The second oldest building on campus, it was the home of the college president in the early days. In front of the building are two sycamore trees said to have been planted in 1766 to commemorate the repeal of the Stamp Act.

The Art Museum
Princeton University
(609) 258-3787
HOURS: Tuesday through Saturday, 10 A.M. to 5 P.M.;
       Sunday, 1 to 5 P.M.

The museum has some of the art works and furnishings of Elias Boudinot, president of the Continental Congress in 1782–83 and a Princeton trustee for nearly fifty years. The Boudinot Rooms re-create the dining room and parlor of Boxwood Hall (see the Elizabeth section of the Union County chapter).

The Princeton Battle Monument
Stockton Street (Route 206) at Nassau Street (Route 27)
(outside Borough Hall)

This fifty-foot-high block of carved Indiana limestone has been called New Jersey's Arc de Triomphe. Some call it a bad imitation of the arc, but most will find it enjoyable just the same. The sculptor was Frederick W. MacMonnies, and the work was unveiled in 1922 by President Warren G. Harding. The figures include Washington leading his troops at the urging of Lady Liberty, and Gen. Hugh Mercer dying a hero's death.

Morven
55 Stockton Street (Route 206)
(609) 683-1514
HOURS: Wednesday, 11 A.M. to 2 P.M.

Morven, a national historic landmark, was the home of Richard Stockton, a signer of the Declaration of Independence. It was started in 1701 by Stockton's grandfather—also named Richard—on land purchased from William Penn. The house was completed in 1755, and Richard Stockton the Patriot inherited it later.

Stockton was captured by the British in 1776 and forced to sign an amnesty agreement, which left his reputation as a Revolutionary War leader in question. Cornwallis used the grand house as his headquarters while pursuing Washington after the Battle of Trenton. His men are said to have dug up three trunks of valuables belonging to the Stockton family from the backyard garden and to have stolen everything, including furniture and other household furnishings. Stockton died at his home in 1781.

Washington was a guest of the family here in 1783 while Congress was in session at Nassau Hall.

Tusculum
166 Cherry Hill Road
(Private)

The residence of John Witherspoon, Princeton's other signer of the Declaration, is on the north side of town. It was taken over by a British infantry division around the time of the Battle of Princeton. According to legend, the invaders—knowing full well that the home belonged to a prominent rebel—vandalized Witherspoon's library and furniture. The house is a large stone structure that cannot be seen from the road except in winter, when the trees on the property are bare.

The Bainbridge House
158 Nassau Street
(609) 921-6748
HOURS: Tuesday, Saturday, and Sunday, noon to 4 P.M.

Built by Richard Stockton, the signer, in 1765, this house was used by members of his family, including Job Stockton, a tanner. William Bainbridge, who was commander of the USS *Constitution* during the War of 1812, was born in the house in 1774.

The British occupied it in late 1776, with Howe using it as a headquarters. In 1783, members of Congress stayed here.

The house today is home to the Princeton Historical Society, which maintains it as a period museum with a fifteen-thousand-volume library on local history and genealogy. Also available are a number of Princeton-area guides and tour maps. One of these, *Follow in Washington's Footsteps,* is a driving tour of some of the Trenton-Princeton Revolutionary War sites.

The Stockton Homestead
32 Edgehill Road
(Private)

This rambling stone house was another Stockton residence that was occupied by British troops. It was known afterwards as the Old Barracks.

The Olden House
344 Stockton Road
(Private)

Legend has it that Washington watched from the porch of this house while his army marched past during the retreat across New Jersey, and that later, following the Battle of Princeton, he revisited the home to instruct his medical staff to give proper care to the British wounded.

Princeton Friends–Quaker Meeting House
470 Quaker Road
(609) 924-5674

This meeting house was used as a hospital during the battle. Richard Stockton is buried in the cemetery.

The Princeton Cemetery
Main Gate on Greenview Avenue

Revolutionary War notables buried in the old part of the cemetery, where Wiggins and Witherspoon Streets meet, include John Witherspoon, signer of the Declaration of Independence; Aaron Burr Sr., one of the Presbyterian leaders of the Great Awakening, which helped establish communication between the independence-minded throughout the colonies; Aaron Burr Jr., vice president of the United States under Thomas Jefferson and killer of Alexander Hamilton; and Judge John Berrien, owner of the house at Rocky Hill where Washington wrote his farewell orders (see the Somerset County chapter). Witherspoon and Burr Sr. were also presidents of Princeton University.

(Note: U.S. President Grover Cleveland is also buried here.)

Trenton

The Trenton Battle Monument
Five Points (junction of Route 31, Route 206, and Princeton
  Avenue)
(609) 737-0623
HOURS: The monument hours have been erratic in the past few
    years, so it's best to call ahead to make sure it is open.

The Trenton Battle Monument overlooks the city from a small hill about six blocks northeast of the state capitol. It's hard to miss, not only because it is one hundred fifty feet high, but because it is at the intersection of five major thoroughfares in the city.

The monument was dedicated on October 19, 1893, the 112th anniversary of the British surrender at Yorktown, an event that many historians believe would not have happened had Washington not routed the Hessians at Trenton. A statue of Washington, his right arm stretched out toward the Delaware River, tops the monument.

The Five Points intersection was no less important during colonial times, and Washington moved his main artillery there to fire down North Warren

Street and North Broad Street on the Hessians. First the Americans had to fight through a Hessian outpost at what today is the intersection of Pennington Avenue and Calhoun Street. Once the guns were in place at the top of the hill, artillery men kept busy, firing repeatedly down the streets and preventing the Hessians from forming lines. One of the officers in charge of the artillery was Alexander Hamilton.

Most of the fighting on this side of the city occurred on the residential streets around Warren and State Streets. Hessian commander Col. Johann Rall was snapped out of a drunken sleep by the sound of gunfire and he got to this area and tried to mobilize his troops. He soon realized that his only chance was to withdraw and regroup, and he ordered a retreat. Seconds later he was mortally wounded by Capt. Frederick Frelinghuysen. The Hessians surrendered shortly after. A plaque on State Street near Montgomery Street marks the spot. The battle, which involved four thousand soldiers fighting mostly hand-to-hand through the neighborhoods, lasted little more than ninety minutes. The number of Hessians captured is estimated at between one thousand and two thousand. Perhaps thirty Hessians were killed, while the Americans suffered no battle deaths.

St. Mary's Cathedral
151 North Warren Street

A plaque on a side wall of St. Mary's Cathedral marks the spot where Colonel Rall was killed.

The American lieutenant James Monroe, who would go on to become the fifth president of the United States, was wounded in this area.

St. Michael's Episcopal Church
140 North Warren Street

Across the street from St. Mary's is St. Michael's Episcopal Church, the oldest church in Mercer County, which Hessian soldiers used as barracks. It was here that Rall failed to organize his men. A plaque on the front of the church says that Washington passed here en route to Boston to take control of the Continental army in 1775.

The First Presbyterian Church
114 East State Street

This church didn't factor directly in the battle, but buried in the cemetery is Abraham Hunt, an unsung hero of the Battle of Trenton. It seems that Hunt, a wealthy merchant, entertained Rall the night before the battle and their heavy toasting left Rall in no condition to lead his troops at daybreak.

But getting drunk wasn't Rall's only mistake. The fifty-five-year-old veteran military man also ignored intelligence that said the Americans were gearing up for an attack; Rall underestimated the enemy, often saying that Washington was an unsophisticated officer commanding an army of farmers and misfits. The irony is this: Howe, recognizing Rall's troublesome traits, had been reluctant to give him a full command. But after Rall performed admirably on the New York battlefields earlier in the year, Howe rewarded him. It was a mistake that cost Rall his life and breathed new life into the Americans.

The Old Barracks Museum

Barrack Street (just south of the State House)
(609) 396-1776
HOURS: Open every day, 10 A.M. to 5 P.M.

On the south side of the city, where Sullivan entered, the fighting began around the Hessians' quarters at the Old Barracks. The Hessians were quickly driven back toward the Assunpink Bridge, where Gen. Arthur St. Clair cut them off.

The fighting on the south side was brutal. The stormy weather made the flintlock muskets useless and the men fought hand-to-hand and with bayonets. Washington had ordered such an attack, telling Gen. John Sullivan, "Use the bayonet. I am resolved to take Trenton."

The Old Barracks Museum is the historical beehive of Trenton. It hosts the annual Battle of Trenton reenactment—an entertaining event that has people in American and Hessian soldier outfits running all around the neighborhood, mimicking the mayhem of the actual fight. The museum offers monthly programs such as "Hessian Occupation Day" and an annual "Sons of the Revolution Flag Disposal Ceremony."

Best of all is watching the staff, dressed as Continental sergeants, put school kids through military drills and show them how to load and fire a cannon as part of the museum's living history program. The cannon boom is one of the regular sounds you hear around the State House.

When the barracks was opened in 1758, it was the biggest building in Trenton, housing British and Irish soldiers stationed in the colonies for the French and Indian Wars. During the Revolution, the Americans moved in first, then the Hessians. After the Hessians were driven out, American soldiers returned. In 1777, the barracks became a Continental army hospital, and the museum now has a room re-created as an authentic Revolutionary War dispensary.

Assunpink Creek Battle (Second Battle of Trenton) Site
Near the bridge on Broad Street

After defeating the Hessians, Washington rounded up his men and the prisoners and crossed back to Pennsylvania. He knew that the British—Cornwallis especially—would be infuriated by his raid on Trenton. Cornwallis had pursued Washington across New Jersey, wanting to punctuate the end of the war with a glorious military victory in the field. Howe was interested in a political solution and felt that Washington's army would simply dissolve.

Now Cornwallis—who had been planning to return to England for a winter leave—was unleashed. He marched his eight-thousand-man army down what today is Route 206 and occupied Princeton for New Year's night. He resumed the mad march the next morning and met opposition led by Col. Edward Hand in Lawrenceville. Hand's delaying action frustrated Cornwallis (see the Lawrenceville section of this chapter), and it took eight hours for the British to march eight miles into Trenton.

Washington meanwhile recrossed the Delaware and dug in across the Assunpink Creek, waiting for Cornwallis. By the time the British entered Trenton it was 4 P.M., and the winter's night darkness was fast approaching.

At the bridge across Assunpink Creek, about where today's bridge is, Washington set up his artillery. His sixteen hundred men loaded their muskets and waited.

Three times Cornwallis's men rushed the bridge. Three times they were repelled by American fire. By then it was too dark to continue fighting. Cornwallis fell back, telling his fellow officers "We'll bag the fox in the morning." His men camped for the night.

Cornwallis had reason to be confident. He had an overwhelming advantage in manpower, and Washington was trapped between the creek and the river.

While the British bedded down Washington held a council of war at the home of Alexander Douglass. He told his officers his plan. They would leave enough men in camp to keep the fires burning, to make the British think the full army was there. But the army wouldn't be there. It would be on its way to Morristown, where Washington planned to spend the winter. In passing Princeton it would make a quick hit there.

Much is made of Washington's playing the "fox" during this time, and in fact much of his time in New Jersey was spent playing hide-and-seek with the British. His attacks at Princeton and Monmouth were on the full British army's rear guard. During the encampments at Middlebrook and Morristown, he never allowed himself to be drawn out of the mountains by British activity. His "baking oven" ruse at Chatham (see the Jacob Morrell House entry in the Chatham section of the Morris County chapter) before the march to Yorktown was legendary. What motivated Washington to fight this way?

First, he knew he could win a war of attrition. If he avoided major casualties or captures and extended the war, it would become prohibitively costly for the king. Wars on foreign soil are expensive.

Second, in New Jersey, where the population seemed evenly divided between Patriots and Loyalists, Washington knew that his much smaller, more mobile army had much less negative impact on the citizens than the huge British machine. Farmers and merchants, who had been indifferent, grew to hate the pillaging invaders who swept the countryside, taking all the food and firewood they could find.

Third—and allow me to speculate—Washington had a personal reason. As a young man, he had been British Gen. Edward Braddock's aide-de-camp during the French and Indian Wars, and had, in fact, buried the general after the Battle of the Wilderness. He had served the British well in those wars and had been named commander of the Virginia militia at age twenty-three. According to Washington biographer James Thomas Flexner, Washington dreamed of a military career as a regular British officer. But the British rebuffed him time and again. He was told he was not regular army material. Washington became demoralized and finally gave up, settling into his Mount Vernon plantation.

No biographer has ever said outright that Washington hated the British, but Flexner documents his frustration in trying to trade with them. When he tried to sell tobacco, the prices offered made it unprofitable. When he tried to trade tobacco for goods, the goods he received were usually substandard.

Washington's role as an early radical was significant, but it was overshadowed by his later accomplishments. He knew earlier than most arch-Patriots that war with England was inevitable.

That said, it must have given Washington enormous, and, yes, basic human pleasure to get England's great generals—Howe, Clinton, Cornwallis—on his own turf and outsmart them.

The Alexander Douglass House
165 East Front Street at Montgomery Street
(609) 989-3111
HOURS: Third Sunday of each month, noon to 4 P.M.

At the time of the Revolution this house was owned by Alexander Douglass, who became quartermaster of the Continental army. Following the December 26 battle with the Hessians, the house was used by Gen. Arthur St. Clair as his headquarters. Washington held a council of war here after the battle at Assunpink Creek on January 2, 1777, during which it was decided that the army would evacuate Trenton later that night, hit the British quickly at Princeton, and press north to the Watchungs. (Note: The sharp-eyed will wonder how Washington was able to use the Douglass house for his council after Assunpink when the house is on the north side of the creek, where the British were. Here's the answer: the house was originally on the south side of the creek, safe behind American lines, at what is today 193 South Broad Street.)

The Trent House
15 Market Street
(609) 989-3027
HOURS: Every day, 12:30 P.M. to 4 P.M. Closed major holidays.

This house has been called one of the finest surviving examples of early eighteenth-century architecture in the country. It was built by William Trent, a wealthy Philadelphia shipowner and merchant, as a summer retreat on the Delaware back when the area was largely uninhabited. Eventually, the area became known as Trent's Town, then Trenton. Trent died in 1726. The house was eventually owned by John Cox, owner of the Burlington County ironworks (including Batsto) which supplied the Continental army with weapons, tools, and ammunition. Before the Battle of Trenton, the house was occupied by Hessian soldiers, who used it as a barracks.

Quaker Meeting House Cemetery
Corner of East Hanover and Montgomery Streets

Buried here are George Clymer, a Pennsylvania signer of the Declaration of Independence; New Jersey Governor Richard Howell, who burned tea at Greenwich (see the Lower Delaware chapter); and Gen. Philemon Dickinson.

Fitch's Gun Shop
North Warren Street

John Fitch was a gun maker who has been called "the official state armorer." When the Hessians occupied Trenton they ransacked his shop. Fitch later invented and ran the first commercial steamboat, seventeen years before Robert Fulton.

Washington's Route Markers

There are a dozen little hidden gems along New Jersey's Revolutionary War trail that mark Washington's route from Trenton to the Battle of Princeton. The twelve stone obelisks were erected by the Sons of the American Revolution in 1914. In some places suburbia sprawls around them, but in others their surroundings have remained undisturbed since they were installed. One sits in the middle of a mall, another in the middle of a cornfield.

Over time, some of the bronze plaques were stolen, but new plaques were eventually made with identical wording: "Route of Washington's march by night from Trenton to Princeton and victory January 3, 1777."

Number One is at the southwest corner of South Broad Street and Hamilton Avenue.

Number Two is seven-tenths of a mile east from Number One, on the left side of Hamilton Avenue.

Number Three is in Hamilton Township, in the vicinity of the intersection of Greenwood and Ward Avenues, near the northwest side of Greenwood Cemetery.

Number Four is near the Mercer County Geriatric Center at Jencohallo Avenue and Chewalla Boulevard (off Nottingham Way) in Hamilton Township.

Number Five is near the Veterans of Foreign Wars Post on Christine Avenue off Klockner Avenue.

Number Six is about two miles away from Number Five, on the left side of Quaker Bridge Road.

Number Seven is one mile north of Number Six off Youngs Road, east of Quaker Bridge Road.

Number Eight is a half mile north on Hughes Drive in the Van Nest Refuge, just west of Quaker Bridge Road.

Number Nine is on Quaker Bridge Road in the Mercer Mall, just north of the intersection with Route 1.

Number Ten is almost two miles north of Number Nine on Quaker Bridge Road, in a wooded area owned by the Institute for Advanced Study in Princeton Township.

Number Eleven is in a cornfield on the right side of Quaker Bridge Road, one mile north of Number Ten.

Number Twelve is in the woods behind the Clark House at Princeton Battlefield State Park.

Middlesex County

Almost all of colonial New Brunswick is gone. Perth Amboy, too. Except for Hudson, no county has as little left as Middlesex. As you will read below, highways and corporate complexes now cover what were extremely important historical sites. The concentrated historic district of New Brunswick now lies under Route 18 and the Johnson & Johnson headquarters. Most of these New Brunswick landmarks went down between the 1930s and the 1960s. Colonial Perth Amboy gave way to an industrial boom much earlier in this century. It's too bad, because these were two very important colonial cities.

Perth Amboy was home to the main body of Washington's "flying camps" and to New Jersey's last royal governor. Its proximity to British-held Staten Island made it strategically important for both sides, and it was the site of ten significant skirmishes.

New Brunswick was a place Washington visited in defeat and in victory: he rested there during his humiliating retreat across New Jersey and again after his inspiring win at Monmouth. For a time in between, the city was occupied by the enemy, and most major British generals spent time there. New Brunswick was strategically important for its access to the Raritan Bay, too, and twenty significant skirmishes occurred there. In one of these, on March 9, 1777, a direct attempt was made on the life of the British commander in chief, Gen. William Howe.

Cranbury

Stites House Site
53 South Main Street

The full British army evacuated Philadelphia in June 1778 and began a march across New Jersey. Washington took his army out of Valley Forge and gave pursuit. On June 26, 1778, Washington arrived in Cranbury, unable to advance the army because of the heat and rain. While the soldiers camped in the area, Washington made his headquarters at the home of Dr. Hezekiah Stites. It is believed that the Marquis de Lafayette, who commanded a number of divisions under Washington, stayed in the house, too.

Legend has it that Aaron Burr hid here in 1804 after the duel in which he killed Alexander Hamilton.

Edison

British Encampment Site
Inman Avenue and Featherbed Lane

In the early morning hours of June 26, 1777, the New Jersey militia began to harass the British troops encamped near here. The British gave chase north into Union County's Ash Swamp, where the soft ground slowed their horses. The Americans took advantage and the first shots of the Battle of Ash Swamp were fired (see the Clark section of the Union County chapter.)

Monroe Township

American Encampment Site
Vicinity of Gravel Hill Road and Monroe Boulevard

After leaving Cranbury, the army camped along the Manalapan Brook in this area. Washington rode to Englishtown that night and ordered Gen. Charles Lee to attack the British early the next morning at Monmouth Court House (see the Shore Counties chapter). Washington then returned to the campsite and met with his generals to plot strategy for the battle the next day.

Washington returned to this camp the night of the battle and, after learning that the British had withdrawn, took his army to New Brunswick.

New Brunswick

Buccleuch Mansion
800 George Street
New Brunswick
(732) 745-5094
HOURS: By appointment.

The British occupied New Brunswick from December 1776 until June 1777, and since this large white mansion was one of the finest houses in town, the redcoats moved in. There is a legend that two officers of the Enniskillen Guards fought a duel in the home and one of them was killed.

Washington stayed here later in the war, when the house was occupied by Col. Charles Stewart, the commissary general of the Continental army.

The house was built in 1739 by Col. Anthony Walton White, who was married to the daughter of a New Jersey provincial governor, Lewis Morris.

White Hall Tavern Site
Albany and Peace Streets

Nothing is left of the tavern, or even of one of the two streets it stood on. Today this is the site of the new Johnson & Johnson headquarters. Progress and the downtown revitalization of New Brunswick have all but destroyed the town's very significant Revolutionary War–era district.

Washington stayed at White Hall, on the north side of Albany Street not far from the Raritan River, on June 23, 1775, while on his way to take command of the Continental army in Massachusetts.

He may have stayed here again on May 22, 1776, while en route from New York to Philadelphia, where he would present his military strategy to Congress, and again on June 5, as he returned to New York. Or he may have stayed across the street at Cochrane's Tavern.

Washington celebrated July 4, 1778, at the White Hall, fresh off his victory at Monmouth. The pamphlet *George Washington in Middlesex County, New Jersey,* by Dr. Richard G. Durnin (see the Research chapter), details the day. Washington's general order of the day went like this:

"Tomorrow the anniversary of the Declaration of Independence will be celebrated by the firing of thirteen pieces of cannon and a feu de joie of the whole line. . . . the soldiers are to adorn their hats with green boughs and to make the best appearance possible. A double allowance of rum will be served out."

The soldiers camped on the Piscataway side of the Raritan River, marched across the old Landing Lane bridge (at approximately the site of the current bridge) and joined the soldiers camped on the bluff overlooking the river on what today is George Street (about where the Rutgers dorms are). Washington reviewed the troops there as they fired their celebratory rounds, and then returned to his headquarters at Ross Hall in Piscataway.

The court-martial of Gen. Charles Lee took place at the White Hall, and the Provincial Congress met here in early 1776, and on two occasions ordered New Jersey men to join forces with the Continental army to help defend New York.

Cochrane's Tavern Site
Albany and Neilson Streets

This building, which was on the southwest corner of this intersection, is gone too. Like White Hall, Peter Cochrane's rambling tavern saw a lot of action during the war.

It was the site of a July 9, 1776, reading of the Declaration of Independence, one of the first in the new nation.

Gen. Charles Lee was held here under house arrest during his court-martial following his apparent insubordination during the Battle of Monmouth (see the Shore Counties chapter). British raider Col. John Simcoe was also held prisoner here after being captured at Franklin (see the Somerset County chapter).

Washington used Cochrane's tavern as headquarters during his retreat across New Jersey in the fall of 1776. The army arrived in New Brunswick on November 29 and pulled out hastily on December 1 as the British were moving in on the city.

Washington's letters to Congress from Cochrane's are filled with the drama and urgency of the situation:

> I am now to inform you that the enemy are still advancing, and that their vanguard has proceeded as far as Bonem, a small town about four miles this side of Woodbridge. . . .
>
> P.S. Half after one o'clock, P.M.—the enemy are fast advancing some of them are now in sight. All of the men of the Jersey flying camp under General Heard . . . refused to continue longer in service.

Later that night, Washington wrote again.

> Half after seven, P.M.—In a little time after I wrote you this evening, the enemy appeared in several parties on the heights of Brunswic. . . . We had a smart cannonade whilst we were parading our men, but without any or but little loss on either side. It being

impossible to oppose them with our present force . . . we shall retreat to the west side of the Delaware . . . where it is hoped we shall meet reinforcement sufficient to check their progress.

Seminary Place Sites
Corner of Seminary Place and George Street

It is believed that Alexander Hamilton led that "smart cannonade," firing down on the British from the bluffs in the vicinity of this intersection. It is also believed that it was around the time of this exchange that Washington met Hamilton, although there is some evidence that Gen. Nathaniel Greene introduced the two earlier in the year. Three months after the New Brunswick encounter, Washington made Hamilton his aide-de-camp and secretary. Hamilton was barely twenty years old.

A twentieth-century painting depicting the cannonade is in Old Queens, the Rutgers administration building on the hill between Somerset and Hamilton Streets near College Avenue.

When Washington retreated from New Brunswick, the British occupied the town and built a small earthworks fort on this site.

Indian Queen Tavern Site
Vicinity of Albany Street and Route 18

Near the White Hall and Cochrane's was another tavern, the Indian Queen or Farquhar House. Benjamin Franklin, John Adams, and Edward Rutledge met here to plot strategy in the days before the Staten Island Peace Conference on September 11, 1776, with Gen. William Howe. Obviously, no agreement was reached at Staten Island.

The building today has been reconstructed at the East Jersey Olde Towne (see the Piscataway section of this chapter).

Guest House Museum
60 Livingston Avenue
(732) 745-5116
HOURS: By appointment.

The Guest House is now part of the public library. It was moved here from its original location on Livingston Avenue and Carroll Place. The museum houses an outstanding permanent Civil War exhibit and other library displays.

Its Revolutionary legend goes like this: Henry Guest, a tanner, hung out a set of hides to dry as the British were about to enter the town. Off in the distance, the British artillery saw these brown hides hanging and thought it was a group of American soldiers. They fired a cannon at the hides, and when the hides did not scatter, they fired again. The British were impressed with the Americans' bravery, but fired again. Then they gave up. Mr. Guest's hides were not damaged in the volley.

Another legend says Thomas Paine hid here from the British, but according to library director Bob Belvin that story has never been documented.

The Neilson House Site
Burnet Street near Route 18

The British commander in chief, Gen. William Howe, had his headquarters here from December 2, 1776, to June 22, 1777. Unfortunately, the house, which was at 265 Burnet, was torn down in the 1870s. Route 18 development in the 1970s obliterated the neighborhood. The house site was actually where Route 18 (northbound) runs today.

Near this house, a post-Yorktown-surrender skirmish between Loyalists and Patriots left five Loyalists dead. The date was January 9, 1782.

Perth Amboy

The Proprietary House
149 Kearny Avenue
(732) 826-5527
HOURS: Wednesday 10 A.M. to 4 P.M.; Sunday 1 P.M. to 4 P.M.

The Proprietary House was home to William Franklin, New Jersey's last royal governor. William Franklin was the son of Benjamin Franklin, the great Patriot and signer of the Declaration of Independence. In the Franklins' case, the acorn not only fell far from the tree, it floated across the Atlantic. William Franklin was unwavering in his support of the British.

He was appointed royal governor in 1763 at the age of thirty-two. As war became inevitable, his father tried on many occasions—including a number of visits to Perth Amboy—to get him to switch his allegiance, but William Franklin remained loyal to the government that had appointed him. Benjamin Franklin regretfully described his son as "a thorough government man."

William Franklin moved to the Proprietary House in 1774 from his home in Burlington because of pressure from the Patriots (see the Burlington County chapter). In Perth Amboy, he felt, he would be among more like-minded British-sympathizers.

But two years later, he was again surrounded by rebellious Americans. On June 3, 1776, Washington established one of his "flying camps" in

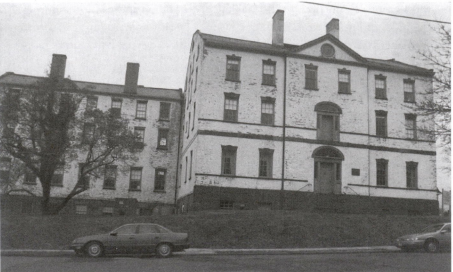

MARK DI IONNO

The Proprietary House, Perth Amboy

Perth Amboy under Gen. Hugh Mercer. This was a contingent of about two thousand men who could be rapidly mobilized to defend the New York area.

On June 10, a contingent from Perth Amboy brought two petitions to New Jersey's Provincial Congress asking that "the government under the king of Great Britain be suppressed and that the . . . [Provincial Congress] establish some more suitable form of government."

The New Jersey Provincial Congress was Franklin's legislative nemesis. The Provincial Congress was formed on May 23, 1775, to prepare the colony for war and to send delegates to the Continental Congress. The Provincial Congress effectively superseded the General Assembly, which was the legislative body under British rule.

On June 15, 1776, the Provincial Congress, meeting in Burlington, ordered the General Assembly to disobey Franklin's order to convene for a new session.

On June 16, the Provincial Congress censured Franklin by a 41-10 vote for ordering the new session. It called him "an enemy to the liberties of this country," suspended his pay, and offered him a choice between parole and arrest. (Note: "Parole" here is used in the literal sense—that a prisoner of war gives his word not to take part in further hostilities in exchange for freedom.)

On June 17, Franklin refused the offer of parole.

On June 18, the Provincial Congress ordered Col. Nathaniel Heard of Woodbridge to arrest Franklin.

On June 19, Franklin was arrested in a midnight raid by Heard and his men.

On June 21, Franklin appeared before the Provincial Congress. That same day, the Provincial Congress voted 53-3 to declare independence from Great Britain.

One June 25, Franklin was sent to East Windsor, Connecticut, where he was imprisoned by order of the Continental Congress.

Franklin was held prisoner there for twenty-seven months. His wife, who witnessed his arrest, was not allowed to visit him. She died while he was in jail. Franklin was released in October 1778 by an American officer, and he returned to New York.

He was named president of the Associated Loyalists, a group of American Loyalists who waged war against their Patriot neighbors. This group was given powers to act on its own, independent of the British military, in raising money, men, and arms. It was also allowed to attack Patriot forces as it saw fit. But after the Joshua Huddy hanging in 1782 (see the Shore Counties chapter), the British commander, Gen. Henry Clinton, stripped the group of its power, and Franklin fled to England. He lived there on a small government pension until he died in 1813.

Shortly after Franklin was taken out of the Proprietary House, Mercer moved in and used it as his headquarters. Mercer and his men joined in Washington's retreat across New Jersey and the house fell into the hands of the British. The British general, William Howe, used it as a headquarters while his troops occupied the area.

The Parker Castle Site
Vicinity of Water and Smith Streets

Until it was demolished in 1942, this three-story clapboard and brick mansion was the oldest house in Perth Amboy (c. 1723). With a commanding view of Raritan Bay, it served a dual purpose—as a lookout spot and a barracks for British soldiers.

St. Peter's Episcopal Church
183 Rector Street (corner of Gordon Street)
(732) 826-1594

The oldest Anglican parish in New Jersey was formed in 1685. While many Anglican churches leaned toward England, St. Peter's was friendly to the rebels.

Perth Amboy Patriots used the church steeple as a watchtower to keep tabs on British and Tory activity across the Arthur Kill and on Staten Island. Early in the war, a small gun was placed in the churchyard and aimed at the British ships. More than once during June 1776, shots were exchanged between the St. Peter's gunners and the British fleet.

 Piscataway

Ross Hall Site
River Road and Ross Hall Boulevard

Washington brought his army to the banks of the Raritan after the Battle of Monmouth. The army camped on both sides of the river—along Johnson Park on the Piscataway side, and along what today is George Street on the New Brunswick side.

Washington stayed at the home of Mrs. Sally Ross, who lived in a mansion with a six-column front porch.

After years of neglect, the mansion was hit by a devastating fire in 1954, and was finally torn down in 1960. A subdivision was built in its place.

Cornelius Low House
1225 River Road
(732) 745-4177
HOURS: Tuesday through Sunday, 1 P.M. to 4 P.M. Closed major holidays.

Cornelius Low, a merchant and attorney of Dutch descent, built a network of warehouses at Raritan Landing, which at that time was a substantial port and trading center in the colonies.

The Revolution split the Low family. One of Low's sons was a Loyalist; another a Patriot. Low himself was neutral, but during the British occupation of New Brunswick, Gen. Charles Cornwallis used his house as his headquarters. He launched the attack on Bound Brook (see the Somerset County chapter) from here, and an American pursuit force brought the fighting to Low's property after the British strike-and-run.

Like all people who lived in occupied areas, Low had very little choice about playing host to Cornwallis. Still, the event left Low's reputation stained. People then—and now—assume he was with the British, not exactly a fair representation. If anything, Cornelius Low just wanted the war to end. The disruption of trade hurt his enterprise at Raritan Landing, and the area was despoiled by armies from both sides. After the war, Raritan Landing was rebuilt and became a thriving river port again, but Low did not live to see it. He died in 1777.

The house now serves as the Middlesex County Museum.

Metlar-Bodine House
1281 River Road
(732) 463-8363
HOURS: Thursday through Saturday, noon to 5 P.M.;
Sunday, 1 P.M. to 4 P.M.

Only two houses from the original Raritan Landing settlement still stand: the Cornelius Low House and the Metlar-Bodine House, which dates back to 1728. The house has no particular Revolutionary War significance except that it witnessed and survived the fighting around it. In the house collection is a cannonball pried out of a tree from a skirmish in the New Market section.

East Jersey Olde Towne
1050 River Road
(732) 745-3030
HOURS: Tuesday through Friday, 8:30 A.M. to 4:15 P.M.;
Sunday, 1:30 to 4 P.M.

In Johnson Park along the Raritan is a collection of eighteenth-century buildings that make up East Jersey Olde Towne.

The reconstructed Indian Queen Tavern is in the village, as is part of one of the Jacobus Vanderveer homes, transported down from Pluckemin.

The remaining Vanderveer House is in Pluckemin on Route 202/206 near River Road (see the Somerset County chapter). That house is believed to have been used by Gen. Henry Knox as his headquarters while he ran the Continental army's artillery school.

However, some historians argue that the Vanderveer house at East Jersey is the real Knox headquarters—or at least part of it. It seems that Jacobus Vanderveer owned two houses. He left one home to one son and the family homestead to another. The family homestead is the house Knox occupied, and it was that house that was moved, in part, to East Jersey.

American Encampment Site
Vicinity of 501 New Market Road

This area, known as Quibbletown during the Revolutionary War, was the site of an American outpost while the British were in New Brunswick. Our Lady of Fatima Church and its school and rectory are on part of the site.

This area of Piscataway is also known as New Market. During the British occupation of New Brunswick there were nine significant skirmishes in the area. Most occurred when foraging parties from both sides, trying to mine the same area, met and fought. On January 16, 1777, four hundred Americans led by Gen. Philemon Dickinson intercepted a British foraging party, captured nine, and left a few dead. On February 20, Americans captured twenty wagons of British food and supplies pilfered from the locals. On March 10, five British soldiers were killed and three Americans wounded in a similar action. Most of this activity occurred in the vicinity of New Market Road and New Brunswick Avenue on the Piscataway–South Plainfield border.

Hendrick Smock House Site
909 River Road (Colgate Palmolive Research Center)

On the Colgate Palmolive property is a vacant nineteenth-century house built on an eighteenth-century foundation. The old foundation is from a house that was in the line of fire during one of the six skirmishes that took place in Piscataway during the winter and spring of 1777, while the British occupied New Brunswick. The foundation has a cannonball indentation in it.

The largest of these battles—and perhaps the only one where artillery was involved—took place on May 17, 1777, when three British regiments attacked Piscataway and Bonhamton. The British reported sixty-seven Americans killed and another one hundred and thirty wounded.

Woodbridge

Cross Keys Inn
142 James Street
(732) 634-9397
HOURS: Unavailable.

Washington stopped at this inn on April 22, 1789, on the way to his inauguration. The original site is on the northwest corner of Main Street, across the street from the Reo Diner and St. James Roman Catholic Church. The Knights of Columbus building is on the spot, and its stone chimney is from the inn.

The inn itself was moved around the corner to James Street and has for years been a private home. It has been altered significantly since Washington's stay. The Woodbridge Historical Association purchased the house in early 1999 and intends to make it a museum.

Like the New Market section of Piscataway, Woodbridge was the site of numerous skirmishes, mostly when the sides clashed during foraging expeditions. Make no mistake: it wasn't only the British who were taking everything off the land. On December 11, 1776, during Washington's retreat through the area, American soldiers made off with four hundred head of cattle and two hundred sheep in one roundup.

During the British occupation of New Brunswick, there were four skirmishes in the area, including one surprise attack at a Woodbridge tavern that killed an American officer and one of his men before the rest of the unit surrendered.

First Presbyterian Church of Woodbridge
600 Rahway Avenue
(732) 634-1024

The Reverend Dr. Azel Roe was a Scottish-born Presbyterian who had no love lost for the English. He was, like James Caldwell, a "fighting parson" who preached independence from the pulpit. He took part in one of the skirmishes at Blazing Star (now Carteret). Later he was captured by the British and held prisoner in New York. Eventually he was returned to his church, where he continued his fifty-two-year tenure as minister.

Roe is buried in the churchyard cemetery, as is Col. Nathaniel Heard, known for arresting the royal governor, William Franklin (see the Perth Amboy section of this chapter). There are about seventy-five other Revolutionary War soldiers buried here, including local legend Nathaniel Fitz Randolph, who died from wounds received at the Battle of Springfield. One story says that when the British tried to capture Fitz Randolph at his home, he answered the door with a loaded pistol in each hand. The British retreated. Another story says that the pockmarks on his gravestone were made by the British or by Loyalists, who peppered his tombstone with musket balls.

Trinity Episcopal Church
Trinity Lane
(732) 634-7422

Next door to the First Presbyterian Church is Trinity Episcopal Church. During the war, this church was decidedly pro-British, and British soldiers were stationed here.

This church cemetery contains the bodies of many Revolutionary War soldiers, including a number of British.

In the church foyer is a display case with Revolutionary War artifacts found on the property, including belt buckles, eating utensils, musket balls, and a cannonball.

Morris County

There is no county in America as important to the Revolutionary War cause as Morris County. Morristown, the county seat then and now, is known as the military capital of the Revolution.

Morris County was not affected by the political ambiguities of other New Jersey counties. Morris was pro-Patriot from the beginning. Following the lead of the most prominent citizens—the Jacob Fords (Jr. and Sr.), Silas Condict, William DeHart, Jonathan Stiles, Benoni Hathaway, to name a few—Morris County residents were among the first in the thirteen colonies to raise a minuteman militia. Two regiments were divided into the Eastern and Western Battalions.

The surrounding hills and the political sympathies teamed to make Morristown Washington's favorite hiding place. He took his army there in the winter of 1777, after successes at Trenton and Princeton, and again in 1779–80. Nestled behind the Watchung Mountains and the Great Swamp, the town was difficult for the British to attack. Yet it was close enough to the main roads between New York and Philadelphia not only to get supplies but also to keep the British in check should they try to penetrate the countryside from their strongholds in New Brunswick and Staten Island.

Both winter encampments gave Washington time to rest his troops and to wrestle more appropriations out of Congress. From his headquarters, first at Jacob Arnold's Tavern, and later at the Ford Mansion, Washington guided the cause through tough times.

It wasn't only its geography that made Morris County ideal. It was its geology, too. Iron deposits throughout the north end of the county, coupled with rapid streams descending graded hills, made it the perfect place for ironworks. There were about a hundred mining operations in the area. Morris County ironworks supplied the Continental army with metal tools, cannons, cannonballs, and musket balls. The foundry and forge at Mount Hope became the biggest single supplier of Revolutionary War ammunition. In addition, Jacob Ford Jr. began one of the first gunpowder mills in the colonies, supplying the army with much-needed explosives.

Chatham

Colonial Historic District
Main Street

On the east end of Chatham's Main Street is the town's colonial historic district. A few revolutionary-era buildings remain on each side of the street.

The Main Street bridge over the Passaic River that leads into the town from Route 124 is essentially where John Day's Bridge was in colonial times. The town was decidedly pro-Patriot, even radical, from the start.

The town was named to honor William Pitt, Earl of Chatham, who spoke out against England's unfair taxation of the colonies. A Liberty Pole—a lightning rod for unwanted British attention—went up on the east side of Day's bridge as early as April 1775—a full fifteen months before the signing of the Declaration of Independence.

Shepard Kollock began printing North Jersey's first newspaper, *The New-Jersey Journal*, from this area. It, too, was decidedly pro-Patriot.

In his book *Shepard Kollock: Editor for Freedom* (see the Research chapter), John R. Anderson indicates that the unbridled rebel spirit made some leaders nervous. Elias Boudinot (see the Union County chapter), who would one day become president of the Continental Congress, sent a letter to the Morris County revolutionary leaders expressing concern about the Liberty Pole:

> We have been much surprised, by Information just received from Mr. Morrell of Chatham given to his Brother of this Town, that there is a determination of a considerable number of your County to raise a Liberty Pole at Chatham tomorrow and from thence they are to proceed to Mr. Thomas Eckley; where it is supposed they intend to offer Violence to his Person on account of some imprudent Expressions said to be inimical to the Liberties of this Country.

It was a good thing for the fledgling nation that Chathamites believed in the cause. The town was the first major settlement on the road from Elizabethtown to Morristown west of Springfield. If Morristown was the military capital of the Revolution, then Chatham was the gateway to the capital. According to Anderson, by 1777 Chatham had become "a militia alarm station, a billeting area for Continental troops and a communications point, for a network of roads fanned out from Chatham, including the courier route to Fishkill on the Hudson."

John Day's Bridge was routinely guarded. In 1776, about three thousand troops under Gen. Charles Lee set up camp there. Washington's army grouped there in August 1781, feigning a buildup for an attack on New York, before marching to Yorktown. It was during that time that Washington stayed at the Morrell House.

The Jacob Morrell House
63 Main Street
(973) 701-9200

While staying with Jacob Morrell, Washington wrote seventeen letters—all dated from Chatham. The last letter, according to John Anderson, detailed his famous oven ruse. Washington wanted the British to believe he was amassing his full force at Chatham to attack the British in New York. He went as far as ordering his men to build giant ovens, the kind capable of baking bread for thousands. Then, in the early morning of August 29, Washington led his men out of Chatham, south to Yorktown. He left a detail of men behind to keep the fires burning to give him more time.

Today, the house is a fine Italian restaurant named Scalini Fedeli. The outside of the building looks much as it did in Washington's day. However, there is no plaque or marker explaining the building's historical significance.

The William Day House
70 Main Street
(Private)

The WPA Guide (see the Research chapter) says a "Day's tavern . . . was frequented by Washington and his officers." That was not the William Day House, but Timothy Day's tavern down near the river. That building burned down in 1965. William Day built his house in 1780. He was a member of the Morris militia for three years, rising to the rank of captain. The house today is in good condition, with an intact beehive oven visible from the east end.

Shepard Kollock Newspaper Site
55 Main Street

A state historical marker has disappeared from this site, where Kollock published the first *New-Jersey Journal* on February 16, 1779. He was called "the rebel printer" by the British, and felt threatened enough during the Battle of Springfield that he dismantled his presses and hid the pieces in separate locations. In 1786, he moved his operation to Elizabethtown (see the Union County chapter). His paper became the *Daily Journal,* and was the oldest active newspaper in the country when it folded in 1992. Kollock died in 1846 at age eighty-eight and is buried in the graveyard at Elizabeth's First Presbyterian Church.

Chatham Township

The Elias Boudinot Home
461 Green Village Road
(Private)

This home, built in the 1760s, was owned by both Lord Stirling and Elias Boudinot, although it is not known if either famous Patriot ever lived there. It is said that the Continental army stored ammunition on the property.

The Isaac Clark Homestead
788 River Road
(Private)

This house appears on a map of the area from 1778 and is said to have quartered Continental army soldiers during the Revolution.

The Lewis Noe Homestead
184 Southern Boulevard
(Private)

Lewis Noe was a lieutenant in the Morris County regiment that survived the brutal winter at Valley Forge.

East Hanover

First Presbyterian Church of Hanover
Mt. Pleasant Avenue at Hanover Road
(973) 887-0298

Like many Presbyterian churches in Morris County, the Hanover church mixed God and politics. This church was the first organized in Morris County (1718). The pastor during the war was the Reverend Jacob Green, who preached independence from the pulpit and was a prolific writer of pro-Patriot articles. Green is said to have redressed a Tory named Eckley during one Sunday service and made him renounce his sinful political ways. Green was influential enough to be an advisor to Washington, and he allowed the church to be used as a hospital after the Battle of Springfield.

Green's home, the Old Parsonage, is a private residence at 27 Hanover Road.

The church cemetery includes the grave of Aaron Kitchell, a three-time member of the House of Representatives and one-time U.S. senator. Kitchell, too, was an advisor to Washington. He served as a pallbearer at his funeral.

At the back of the cemetery is the unmarked mass grave of forty British soldiers who died of smallpox.

Halfway House
174 Mt. Pleasant Ave.
(973) 428-8200
HOURS: By appointment.

This Revolutionary-era tavern was the home of Col. Ellis Cook, a member of the Morris County militia. It was nicknamed the Halfway House because it was approximately halfway on the route the farmers of West Jersey traveled in taking their goods to market in Newark. At this writing, the house is being renovated and furnished by the East Hanover Historical Society, with plans to be complete by winter of 2000. The rooms will be outfitted to reflect different times in East Hanover history, but one will be a replica of the taproom during the days of Cook's tavern.

Florham Park

Hedges-Fish Homestead
202 Brooklake Road
(Private)

Built in 1751, this farm contracted to sell oats to the Continental army in 1779. There are three homes on the property straddling Brooklake Road. The home that has the historical marker in front looks abandoned and in disrepair. Behind the main house is a collection of antique farm equipment. Brooklake Road today is a well-trafficked suburban road with many newer homes, but it is interesting to see a number of colonial-era homes like the Homestead in the area.

Harding Township

Peter Kemble House
667 Mt. Kemble Avenue (Route 202)
(Private)

This house was originally located at the corner of what is now Route 202 and Tempe Wick Road, but it was moved slightly north in 1840. The house was built by Peter Kemble, who owned the mountain that shadows the highway here and which now bears his name. Kemble had strong political ties to England and his daughter was married to Gen. Thomas Gage, the one-time commander of the British army in America. At one point, Kemble was a Loyalist, but he later had Washington and other officers to dinner on perhaps more than one occasion. His house was also used as a headquarters for the American generals William Smallwood and "Mad" Anthony Wayne.

This stretch of road leading into Morristown also includes a cluster of other houses from the Revolutionary War era. It's hard to understand why it hasn't been designated a historic district.

Washington's Route Markers

These tombstone-size markers trace the escape route Washington took from Trenton to Morristown following the Battle of Trenton on Christmas Day 1776. He arrived in Morristown on January 6, 1777, for his first winter encampment there.

There are two markers in Harding Township. The first is on a grassy island at the New Vernon crossroads, where Blue Mill Road becomes Lee's Hill Road and Village Road turns into Glen Alpin Road (which becomes Tempe Wick Road if you follow it west). The other is east on Village Road (toward Green Village), where it intersects with Spring Valley Road and Dickson's Mill Road.

These two markers were placed by the Daughters of the American Revolution in 1933. There are similar markers in Mercer and Somerset Counties.

Kinnelon Borough

Charlotteburg Forge Site
Route 23 South, near Smoke Rise entrance

This Revolutionary War forge had connections with the three biggest names in the New Jersey iron industry: it was built by Peter Hasenclever and later managed by John Jacob Faesch (see the Rockaway Township section of this chapter) and Robert Erskine (see the Passaic County chapter).

There were three forges along about a two-mile stretch of the Pequannock River, a furnace, and a village. All are gone. A marker stands on the approximate site of the village.

Lincoln Park

John Dod's Tavern
8 Chapel Hill Road

Right off of Route 202 in downtown Lincoln Park is Chapel Hill Road. A half block in is the original John Dod's Tavern, which now houses dentists' offices. The stone building has a historical marker out front, which explains that the tavern was a popular stop for Washington and other Continental army officers on the much-used route between Morristown and West Point.

If you follow Chapel Hill Road east it eventually turns into Two Bridges Road. Near the spot where the Pompton River flows into the Passaic is Millington Park, where parts of the Continental army frequently camped. The site is unmarked.

Long Hill Township

Sentinel Elms and Beacon Site
Long Hill Road and Central Avenue
(Private)

Now owned by the Trinity Ministry Center, Sentinel Elms was the home of Cornelius Ludlow, a colonel in the Morris County militia.

Across the street, the Long Hill Township Historical Society plans to put up a monument at the site of the town's signal beacon. During the war, Washington placed a series of signal beacons along the high points of the Watchungs and other mountains in New Jersey and up the Hudson to warn of encroaching British troops. Very few of these have been located exactly. (See the Summit section of the Union County chapter.)

East of these sites at the intersection of Long Hill Road and Hickory Tavern Road is a colonial house that local legend says is haunted by a Hessian horseman. The house (a private home) was a stage stop during the war.

Madison

The Sayre House
31 Ridgedale Avenue
(Private)

Built in 1745 by Daniel Sayre, this saltbox home was opened to officers and soldiers during the Loantaka encampment in 1777. Gen. "Mad" Anthony Wayne used it as his headquarters. Nearby are garden apartments and a street named for the colorful general (as is the Passaic County town of Wayne). The sign in front of this plain, drab olive house says the Reverend James Caldwell (see the Union County chapter) was a frequent visitor. There are a number of other small houses along this road dating back to the 1740s.

The Luke Miller House
105 Ridgedale Avenue
(Private)

This house, built in 1730 by Andrew Miller, is in excellent condition. Miller's son Josiah, a blacksmith and farmer, opened the home to Continental soldiers encamped in the Loantaka Valley. Luke Miller, Josiah's son, was a major in the Morris County militia and lived in the house until his death at age ninety-one.

Mendham

Hilltop Church
Hilltop and Talmadge Roads
(973) 543-4012
HOURS: By appointment.

The First Presbyterian Church in Mendham is an impressive structure. Set on a hilltop just a few blocks south of Main Street (Route 124), the church's 130-foot steeple is one of the highest points in Morris County. The simple white clapboard church has six two-story windows on each side. From the graveyard behind the church, the views north and east are long-range. The whole package is New England postcard pretty—a testament to New Jersey's own rural beauty.

Buried in the church cemetery are twenty-seven Continental soldiers who died during the smallpox epidemic that swept through the winter encampment at Jockey Hollow 1779–80.

The church was used as a hospital during the epidemic. The Reverend Thomas Lewis, the pastor there, cared for the ailing men. He, too, contracted the disease; he died in August. Behind the church is a monument to Lewis and the men. Lewis's grave site is nearby.

The current church—built in 1860—is the fourth church on the hilltop. Two of the previous three were struck by lightning and burned down.

Lebbeus Dod House
67 West Main Street
(Private)

Lebbeus Dod was a captain in the Morris militia, but was also one of the finest precision craftsmen in the colonies. His clocks, timepieces, and mathematical and surveying instruments were second to none. The house on West Main doubled as his workshop.

 Montville

Henry Doremus House
490 Main Road (Route 202, Towaco section)
(973) 334-8487
HOURS: To be determined.

This small stone house—the size of most garages today—appears on Revolutionary War maps of the area. Washington stayed here on June 25 and 26, 1780, after the Battle of Springfield. Also, American and French troops camped in the extensive orchards surrounding the house on August 27, 1781, on their way to Yorktown. Those orchards now house the Hunting Hills townhouse development.

The house is owned by the town of Montville and, at this writing, is undergoing a complete renovation funded by the town and the nonprofit Doremus House Restoration Fund.

"We're hoping to make it an educational facility for kids and adults," said Lorraine Crevaux, president of the fund. Crevaux said the house will be completely restored and furnished to reflect the Revolutionary War period.

Morristown

The town has been called the military capital of the Revolution since an Act of Congress in 1933 made Morristown the nation's first national historical park. The park was dedicated, appropriately, on July 4, 1933.

The park includes more than a thousand acres of historic lands in downtown Morristown and at Jockey Hollow, three miles southwest, which straddles Harding, Mendham, and Morris Townships. (Jockey Hollow is being included here in the Morristown section for continuity's sake.)

The park has four separate components: Washington's Headquarters at the Ford Mansion, Fort Nonsense, Jockey Hollow, and the nearby New Jersey Brigade Encampment Area. The Ford Mansion and Jockey Hollow both have interpretive centers and exhibits. Fort Nonsense and the Jersey Brigade area are just nice open spaces. All are operated and maintained by the National Park Service.

The Ford Mansion and Museum
230 Morris Avenue
(973) 538-2085
HOURS: Daily, 9 A.M. to 5 P.M., except Thanksgiving, Christmas, and New Year's Day.

The Ford Mansion is the most famous of the many "Washington's Headquarters" in the Mid-Atlantic states.

In 1774 Jacob Ford Jr. began construction of the finest mansion in Morris County. But he never saw it completed. He and his father died in 1777. The younger Ford's widow, Theodosia, lived there with four young children. In 1779, George Washington moved in with his cadre of officers—including Alexander Hamilton—and his 150-man elite Life Guard, who built fourteen temporary shelters on and around the property. Martha Washington came to stay, too, escorted by a nephew, George Augustine Washington. Washington received Count Casimir Pulaski here, as well as the Marquis de Lafayette, who told him the French were coming to help the American cause.

Washington arrived on December 1, 1779, during an ice storm. The storm was a sign of things to come: the winter unfolded as one of the worst on record, with twenty-eight winter storms making life for men camped at Jockey Hollow an icy hell. They were badly clothed and ill fed. They faced a smallpox epidemic. ("Dead Carcasses in and about Camp are to be buried by fatigue partys from the Brigade near which they lay," Washington wrote on February 20 in his general orders.)

The Washington Association of New Jersey purchased the property in 1873 and turned it into a museum, which accounts for its pristine condition and authentic furnishings. Over the years, the association has purchased and returned to the house a number of items and furnishings that Washington used there.

Like the state parks at Fort Lee and Washington Crossing, the museum behind the Ford Mansion is the best place to go to see wartime weapons,

Washington Statue outside the Ford Mansion, Morristown

uniforms, and other memorabilia. The Morristown museum does the best job of explaining the New Jersey politics of the Revolution, and its weapons collection is outstanding. Among the highlights are two swords owned by Washington and the "Old Sow" cannon of Battle of Springfield fame (see the Union County chapter).

One of the best items in the museum collection is the suit Washington wore to his inauguration, but it is only displayed on special occasions.

Fort Nonsense
Off Ann Street (behind the Morris County Courthouse)

Even the great Washington wasn't exempt from sarcasm from the troops. In May 1777, he had his men build a giant earthworks fort—a system of deep trenches behind dirt and wood embankments—on the highest hill in Morristown, overlooking the Green. The plan was to build a refuge that soldiers and citizens alike could get to safely in case of British attack, with cannons pointing east and south (the directions the British would be coming from.)

However, Washington pulled out of Morristown for Middlebrook at the end of the month and the fort was never used. Soldiers grumbled that the fort was built just to keep them busy. It was later nicknamed Fort Nonsense.

The fort today is part of the Morristown National Historical Park. It has all-weather information boards explaining the layout of the fort and the way it was built. The view, of course, remains as spectacular as it was in Washington's day.

Jockey Hollow
North entrance off Western Avenue in Morris Township
South entrance off Tempe Wick Road in Harding Township
HOURS: Daily, 9 A.M. to 5 P.M., except Thanksgiving, Christmas, and New Year's Day.

Washington picked the site of the Jockey Hollow encampment by himself. It was protected by hills and remote enough so that the men there would not overrun Morristown. Ten to twelve thousand men encamped there during the 1779–80 winter, and a smaller contingent returned for the winter of 1780–81.

Jockey Hollow is prime New Jersey countryside: rolling hills, winding roads, smooth hiking trails. A tour road takes you past all the significant sites. In any season, it is a beautiful place, although it's hard to beat autumn in this part of the state. A walk through the park on a steely-skied February day will give you an idea of how cold and windblown Washington's men must have felt.

The hardships at the camp are legendary. Many of the men had no shoes and wrapped rags around their feet to keep them from freezing. They arrived in snow and began logging to make their huts, working with bare feet and legs in a foot of snow. Food was scarce and many men bolted camp to steal from neighboring farms. Thieves were routinely given a hundred lashes, but hunger is a stronger motivator than pain is a deterrent, and the crime spree continued. Washington himself wrote that men were eating "every kind of horse food except oats." He had horses taken out of camp because there was no food for them.

In all, there were eight infantry brigades, including men from New Jersey, Pennsylvania, Maryland, Connecticut, New York, and Rhode Island. They spent most of their days huddled around fires except when drilling on the Grand Parade Grounds near the north end of the park.

The most experienced soldiers at Jockey Hollow were two thousand men of the Pennsylvania Line, who were housed on Sugar Loaf Hill.

A plaque near Sugar Loaf Hill lauds the Pennsylvanians as "the backbone of Washington's army. From the invasion of Canada of 1775 to the victory at Yorktown in 1781 Pennsylvania troops served in almost every major battle."

During the second Jockey Hollow encampment, the war-weary Pennsylvanians, who hadn't been paid in a year, decided to march armed to Philadelphia to exact some funds from Congress. A loyal group of soldiers made an attempt to stop the mutineers, and in the ensuing fight Capt. Adam Bettin was killed. His grave is beside the tour road near the Grand Parade Grounds. (The situation was later resolved by the mutineers' commander, "Mad" Anthony Wayne.)

On Sugar Loaf Hill today are five replica soldier huts. The accommodations could be called shelter and nothing more. Just south of the huts at the bottom of the hill is a boulder with a plaque marking the spot of the Jockey Hollow Cemetery, where one hundred soldiers are supposed to be buried.

According to Eric Olsen, a historian/ranger at the park, the plaque is probably wrong.

> They did an archaeological dig there in the 1930s when the park was created and found nothing but a bullet extractor and a bullet that had been bitten down on [the favored method of anesthesia in camp]. Based

on that, some people think there was a hospital here, but we know the hospital was in Basking Ridge [see the Somerset County chapter]. The idea of military cemeteries didn't become fashionable until the Civil War. During the Revolution, if you died in battle they basically buried you where you fell. Or they dug a mass grave near the battle-field, which they never marked. If you died in camp they buried you on the parade ground, but they never marked the graves because they didn't want the spies to do a head count.

At the south end of the park is the Tempe Wick House. During the Revolution it was the centerpiece of a fourteen-hundred-acre farm owned by Henry Wick, a cavalryman with the Morris County militia and a member of Governor Livingston's guard unit. But for all of Henry Wick's accomplishments, he was upstaged by his daughter, Tempe (Temperance) during the Pennsylvania Line mutiny.

Legend has it that a group of mutineers tried to commandeer her horse. She at first appeared ready to dismount, then wheeled the horse and took off. When she arrived at home she hid the horse in her bedroom. The soldiers came along and searched the stables and barn, then left without the steed.

Over time, the legend grew to mythic proportions. One story claimed she kept the horse in the house for three weeks. Another said that she put her featherbed down on the floor so the soldiers wouldn't hear the horse hoofs on the wood.

Eric Olsen doesn't believe any of it.

"We tend to doubt it very much," he said. "The story didn't appear in print until the 1870s, after Tempe Wick and her husband and children were all dead. The author of that story didn't say where he got his facts from. We know that a lot of bad history can be traced back to the nineteenth century. They tended to make stuff up. As for the horse-in-the-house-for-three-weeks story, all I can say is a horse makes about forty-five pounds of manure a day. If you do the math. . . ."

Another house still standing on the property is the Joshua Guerin House at the north entrance to the park. Guerin was a sergeant in the Morris County militia. He was a wagon driver and a blacksmith. The house today is used by the park service and is not open to the public.

From Jockey Hollow, follow signs to the New Jersey Brigade area, which doubles as a wildlife sanctuary. Nine hundred New Jerseyans, the last to arrive in the winter of 1779, built nearly one hundred simple log huts in this area.

The Green

At the center of Morristown, where Route 202 meets Route 124, is the Green. It has been the town center since the early 1700s. During the winter encampment of 1777, Washington made his headquarters on the Green at Arnold's Tavern, a three-story structure that survived until 1918. A sign marks the spot of the tavern on the west side of the Green in front of 20 North Park Place.

Washington arrived at Arnold's Tavern on January 6, 1777, fresh from his surprise-attack victory at Trenton on Christmas and his hit-and-run win at Princeton. His troops were tired and in need of fresh provisions and uniforms.

Unlike the brutal winter encampment at Jockey Hollow three years later, the "Loantaka Encampment" of 1777 did not cause excessive hardship. The winter was milder and—according to the book *In Lights and Shadows: Morristown in Three Centuries,* by Cam Cavanaugh (see the Research chapter)—Washington put his officers and men "in every house and barn in the vicinity, including Hanover, Whippany, Chatham and Madison. A good-sized encampment is believed to have pitched tents in the Loantaka [Spring] Valley." The location of the main camp remains a mystery, although it is believed to be close to the intersection of Woodland and Treadwell Avenues in Chatham Township, near the convergence of Madison Borough, Harding Township, and Morris Township.

Washington's stay at Arnold's was marked by three important events.

First, he organized a spy network and put Alexander Hamilton in charge of intelligence. He also instituted the policy of falsifying reports of manpower, weapons, supplies, and ammunition to fool the British into thinking the army was much healthier than it was in reality.

Second, he began a crackdown on Tories and Loyalists. Until this time, Washington had left civilians out of the political tug-of-war for loyalties. Now he wanted Americans to sign a pledge of allegiance or risk losing property.

Third, he took a chance with experimental medicine and ordered his men to be immunized against smallpox. The men were injected with a mild case of the disease to build up an immunity. This was risky at best, but it worked and the army had a lower mortality rate than the civilian population.

Washington himself took ill at Arnold's, coming down with a severe throat ailment. Martha Washington visited during this period, one of the rare times she followed her husband into the field (see the Ford Mansion entry in the Morristown section of this chapter).

The tavern stood on the Green until 1886, when it was moved to Mt. Kemble Avenue, where it became All Souls Hospital. It burned down in 1918.

Near Arnold's Tavern was the Continental storehouse (on the site of Epstein's department store today). Supplies such as weapons, food, uniforms, tents, and tools were kept there. Washington had his men roll barrels of sand in and out of the warehouse to give British spies the impression that the army was flush with provisions.

On the north side of the Green is the First Presbyterian Church. Founded in 1733, the church was rebuilt in 1791 and again in the 1890s. Washington attended services there while in Morristown. The cemetery holds the bodies of a number of Revolutionary War soldiers and other figures, such as ironmaster John Jacob Faesch (see the Rockaway Township section of this chapter).

Site of the Dickerson (or Norris) Tavern
Spring Street and Martin Luther King Boulevard

The court-martial of Benedict Arnold took place at the Dickerson Tavern between December 23, 1779, and January 26, 1780, but it had nothing to do with the treason he later committed. Instead it was about his abuse of power for personal profit during the British evacuation of Philadelphia in 1778. Arnold was found guilty on two counts and his punishment was a public reprimand by Washington. That spring (1780), Washington, still unaware that Arnold had been an agent for the British since April 1779, gave him command of West Point, which Arnold would eventually attempt to hand over to the British.

The Thomas Paine Monument
Burnham Park
Washington Street

About a half mile from the Green as you travel west on Washington Street is the Thomas Paine Monument. This impressive statue is the centerpiece of Burnham Park, a nice little roadside stop with a pond and a few picnic tables. Paine is depicted with a quill pen in one hand and a flintlock gun at rest in his lap. The marble block is inscribed with some of Paine's independence-inspiring prose.

Artillery Park
Washington Street

A few hundred feet down the road west of Burnham Park is Artillery Park, which consists of a bench, a flagpole, and two plaques, one set in a boulder.

During the encampment at Jockey Hollow, the Continental army artillery under Gen. Henry Knox was here. The soldiers were housed in huts along the steep hillside beyond the park. The road was lined with cannons, and the horses were stabled at Burnham Park.

Schuyler-Hamilton House
5 Olyphant Place
(973) 267-4039
HOURS: Sunday, 2 P.M. to 5 P.M.

Owned and maintained by the Daughters of the American Revolution, this house is where the romance between Alexander Hamilton and Betsy Schuyler blossomed.

While Washington maintained headquarters at the Ford Mansion Hamilton was his aide-de-camp. Betsy Schuyler was the niece of Dr. John Cochrane, the surgeon general of the army and Washington's personal physician, who was using the Olyphant Place house as his headquarters.

It is not known exactly when Hamilton met Betsy Schuyler, but he visited frequently while she was at the house. A few months later they were engaged, then married.

The house is outfitted with furnishings from the period and portraits of Betsy Schuyler and Alexander Hamilton.

Morris Plains

Ebenezer Stiles House
77 Glenbrook Road
(973) 683-1089
HOURS: The museum is open Saturday, 10 A.M. to 1 P.M.

Continental army light horsemen stayed here at times during the war and stabled their horses on the surrounding grounds. The house today is the Morris Plains Public Library and Morris Plains Museum. It is surrounded on three sides by pleasant little Roberts Park.

Parsippany

Livingston-Benedict House
25 Parsippany Road
(Private)

William Livingston, the commander of the New Jersey militia and first governor of the state, lived at Liberty Hall outside Elizabethtown (see the Union County chapter).

He was a powerful and influential leader of the rebels, and therefore the British hated him. According to *Union County Yesterday* (see the Research chapter), Livingston survived " 'repeated attempts by the British and the Loyalists to capture him. In 1778 a reward of two thousand guineas and a pension from the crown of Great Britain during life' was offered for 'that damned rascal Governor Livingston' dead or alive. It is said that he did not sleep more than two consecutive nights in the same place; and he was seldom able to visit his beloved Liberty Hall."

One of Livingston's hiding places was this home, which was safely far from the British forces, spies, and Loyalists of his home county and close to Morristown and the protection of Washington's army. Livingston narrowly escaped a kidnaping attempt while staying here, according to some sources: a group of Loyalists surrounded the house at night, waiting to waylay him at daybreak, but Livingston sneaked past them in the dark.

Forge Pond
Off Troy Road

In Revolutionary War times, Forge Pond was the site of an ironworks where cannonballs for the army were made. The ironworks was part of a small industrial town called Troy, where a sawmill and gristmill also operated.

As of this writing, the pond is dry. The Department of Environmental Protection ordered it drained in 1994 because the existing dam was ruled unsafe.

The 10-acre pond and the 130 acres of wetland around it are owned by a developer who wants to build 120 homes off Troy Road. (The proposed development will be called Parkside Gardens.) The developer wants to deed the pond and the surrounding area back to the town, but the town wants him to build a new dam and restore the pond first.

Rockaway Borough

Stephen Jackson House
40 East Main Street
(Private)

George Washington was surrounded by an elite squadron called the Life Guard. New Jerseyan Stephen Jackson, a captain, was a member of the guard.

The large, white-columned house is today part of the Sacred Heart School. It is divided in two: part of it serves as a convent for the nuns, and the other part is the school library, music room, and computer room.

Rockaway Presbyterian Church
Church Street (Route 513)

This pretty little brick church was built in 1832 to replace the original meeting house, which was established in 1758. The church was a meeting place and safe haven for firebrand speakers who preached revolution. The grave of William Wind, a general in the New Jersey militia, is on a knoll directly behind the church.

Rockaway Township

Ford-Faesch Manor House
Mt. Hope Road near the entrance to the Mt. Hope Quarry (past Garden Road)
(973) 829-8666
HOURS: To be determined.

Built by Jacob Ford Jr. (see the Morristown section of this chapter) around 1768, this was the manor house of John Jacob Faesch's Mount Hope Furnace ironworks. Faesch was a Swiss mining engineer and one of the colonies' best ironmasters. His seven-hundred-acre plant made cannons and ammunition for the army. Washington liked the products so much he sent captured Hessians to work in Faesch's forge, and he exempted Faesch's other employees from the draft. For most of the war, Faesch's ironworks was Washington's biggest supplier of cannons, cannonballs, shells, and other guns and ammunition.

When the war ended, Faesch's business began to falter. He died in 1799 and is buried at the Presbyterian Church on the Morristown Green.

The stone house, which sits on a hill overlooking Mount Hope Pond and the Mount Hope Quarry, was abandoned in the mid-1970s and fell into disrepair while the deed was in limbo. The town eventually acquired it and, as of this writing, is extensively renovating it. The work is partially underwritten by a grant from the New Jersey Historic Trust.

"This has been a twenty-year project," said Donald M. Erickson, a volunteer in the restoration. "We just got the building stabilized so it's safe for us to work in there now."

Mount Hope Furnace was just one of the many ironworks in northwestern New Jersey (see the Long Pond Iron Works and Ringwood Manor entries in the Passaic County chapter). Not too far from Mount Hope is the unmarked site of Hibernia Furnace, another supplier of munitions to the army, which was owned by Lord Stirling.

It's interesting to note that the military industry continues in the area today. Just over the ridge is the eastern border of Picatinny Arsenal, a U.S. Army weapons development facility. At the Rockaway Township municipal building on Mt. Hope Road is an exhibit about the industry, which includes a time line showing the evolution of these businesses.

Roxbury Township

The First Presbyterian Church of Succasunna
99 Main Street (Succasunna section)
(973) 584-5238
HOURS: By appointment.

This church, built in 1853, stands on the site of the original, which was used as a storehouse for captured British arms during the war. The church also served as a hospital for soldiers encamped at Morristown who fell ill in a smallpox epidemic during the winter of 1779–80. Those who died are buried in the church cemetery along with Mahlon Dickerson, governor of New Jersey (1815) and secretary of the navy (1834).

It's interesting to note that the red historical marker out front, placed by the Morris County Heritage Commission, uses the archaic spelling of the place name. On the sign, the church is described as the First Presbyterian Church at Suckasunny Plains.

Stone House Farm (also known as the Lewis Cary House)
208 Emmans Road (Ledgewood section)
(Private)

Soldiers with smallpox were sent to this house when the church infirmary got overcrowded. Those who died are buried on the property.

Washington Township (Long Valley section)

The Philip Weise House
25 East Mill Road (Route 24)
(Private)

Nicknamed "The Fort," the stone Weise house, built in 1774, was a storage place for Continental army goods. It also housed soldiers.

Passaic County

As part of the iron belt that also reaches into neighboring Morris County, Passaic County was important not only for supplies but also as a transportation corridor. Washington came through here with his army a number of times, staying at the Dey Mansion in what today is Wayne and also at Ringwood with his friend and chief mapmaker, Robert Erskine.

Bloomingdale

Site of New Jersey Line Mutiny
Federal Hill (off Union and Van Dam Avenues)

The year 1780 was a winter of discontent in the Continental army. Members of the Pennsylvania Line mutinied at Morristown on January 1, marching off to Philadelphia to confront Congress over unpaid wages (see the Morris County chapter). At about the same time, about one hundred men from Massachusetts regiments called it quits at West Point and began marching home. Members of the New Jersey Line also mutinied.

In the first two cases there were peaceful resolutions (although Gen. "Mad" Anthony Wayne, who retrieved his Pennsylvanians at Princeton, ordered the hanging of a British spy who tried to get the men to defect).

The men who led the New Jersey Line mutiny weren't so lucky. On January 20, the two hundred New Jerseyans camped at Pompton began a march to Chatham to persuade the three hundred New Jersey Brigade members there to join them in a mutiny. The brigade commander, Israel Shreve, convinced the mutineers instead to return to Pompton.

Washington, at West Point, heard of the mutiny, and dispatched six hundred loyal troops with three cannons to put down the uprising. Washington himself went to Ringwood to keep an eye on the situation.

The men who returned to Pompton were disorderly and insubordinate until faced with superior fire power. Then they obeyed an order to assemble without arms. At that point, officers made the men submit the names of the worst agitators, and three were picked by lottery to be shot by a firing squad of other mutineers. Sergeants George Grant, David Gilmore, and John Tuttle were selected to die, but Grant got a last-minute reprieve. The other two did not, and they were executed on Federal Hill in Bloomingdale on January 27, 1781. A historical marker here tells the story.

Passaic

Washington Crossing Site
Main Avenue Bridge (into Wallington)

On November 21, 1776, Washington and his army crossed the Passaic River with the British in pursuit during the retreat across New Jersey. The Americans burned the bridge behind them to slow the British, then turned south and headed down the west bank of the Passaic into Newark.

There is a blue-and-silver plaque on the Wallington side of the bridge (see the Bergen County chapter) telling the story of the event. However, the plaque has the date wrong. It says November 21, 1777.

Paterson

The Great Falls
McBride Avenue at Spruce Street
The Great Falls Visitors' Center
65 McBride Avenue
(973) 279-9587
HOURS: Monday through Friday, 9 A.M. to 4 P.M.;
Saturday, noon to 4 P.M. Closed Sunday.

Washington and his entourage, which included Alexander Hamilton, stopped at the base of the seventy-foot falls on July 10, 1778.

Thirteen years later, as President Washington's secretary of the treasury, Hamilton set in motion a plan for an American manufacturing city that could harness the power of those falls. Seven hundred acres around the falls were purchased by the Society for Establishing Useful Manufactures, in which Hamilton was a driving force, to create the mill town that Paterson eventually became.

You can park at the visitors' center and walk to a viewing spot above the falls.

Ringwood

Ringwood Manor
Sloatsburg Road
(973) 962-7031
HOURS: Wednesday through Sunday, 10 A.M. to 3:30 P.M.
        Outdoor areas open daily, dawn till dusk.

Ringwood State Park is a five-thousand-acre retreat in the middle of the Ramapo Mountains. The current manor house was completed in 1879: it has fifty-one rooms on three floors, twenty-eight bedrooms, twenty-four fireplaces, thirteen bathrooms, a handful of parlors and drawing rooms, and two hundred fifty windows.

MARK DI IONNO

Robert Erskine Grave Site, Ringwood Manor

Robert Erskine Plaque, Ringwood Manor

It is filled with artwork and artifacts from the Victorian Age, and is considered a premier example of industry-magnate opulence of the day.

However, its Revolutionary War significance centers around a man who was anything but ostentatious.

Robert Erskine became the ironmaster at Ringwood in 1771, when he took over for John Jacob Faesch, who moved on to Mount Hope (see the Morris County chapter).

Erskine sided with the Patriots when war broke out, organizing his workers into a militia, of which he was captain. They were kept on the job at the forge, however, turning out ordnance and camp stoves and banging out links of the great chain that was used to keep British ships from going up the Hudson. (Replicas of that chain are displayed outside at the Manor House.)

But Erskine was also a skilled engineer in hydraulics and topography, and he became the official surveyor and geographer for Washington—a trained surveyor himself, who understood the strategic imperative of knowing the lay of the land.

Erskine made 129 maps for Washington, many of New Jersey. They show not only the roads and the topography but also the homes in the area (and the names of their owners). Many of these maps today are the property of the New-York Historical Society.

Erskine's work was not highly publicized during or after the war, but his maps were critical to Washington, helping him make informed choices about troop movement.

Washington liked Erskine. He visited him at Ringwood several times as he traveled between West Point and Morristown. When Erskine died suddenly after catching pneumonia on a mapmaking expedition, Washington went to Ringwood for his funeral.

Erskine is buried at the park, a few hundred yards south of the Manor House. There is a legend about an eerie blue light that emanates from his grave, and some have claimed to see the ghost of Erskine in the area.

Cannonball Run
Skyline Drive Vicinity

Just before the Skyline Drive exit on Route 287 there is a walking-trail overpass with a sign that says "Cannonball Run."

This was the name of a secondary road used by Patriots who did not want to be detected by Tories along the main roads. Supplies, weapons, and ordnance were moved along this road, which went in a circular path along the ridge of Ramapo Mountain (on today's Skyline Drive), through Long Pond, and up toward Sloatsburg, New York.

Totowa

Continental Army Encampment Site

During July, October, and November 1780, Washington brought his army to the area then known as Preakness. While Washington stayed at the Dey Mansion (see the Wayne section of this chapter) his men camped along the Passaic from what is now Laurel Grove Cemetery on River View Road in Totowa all the way up to the Goffle Road area in Hawthorne.

Wayne

The Dey Mansion
199 Totowa Road
(973) 696-1776
HOURS: Wednesday through Friday, 1 P.M. to 4:30 P.M.; Saturday
and Sunday, 10 A.M. to noon and 1 P.M. to 4:30 P.M.

Washington used the house of Theunis Dey, a colonel in the Bergen County militia, as his headquarters while his troops camped in the Preakness Valley.

Washington stayed here while his troops were maneuvering in Bergen County, throughout the Hackensack Valley, and in what today is Hudson County. From here he helped plot Gen. "Mad" Anthony Wayne's failed attack on Bull's Ferry (see the Essex and Hudson Counties chapter), had a hand in the Marquis de Lafayette's futile attack on Staten Island, and abandoned plans to make a major assault on New York.

In typical Washington fashion, he took over the home. His 150-man Life Guard camped in and around the house. Lafayette, Lord Stirling, Alexander Hamilton, Nathaniel Greene, and Benedict Arnold all stayed there at one time or another. Washington wrote a remarkable seven hundred letters from here.

The house today is owned and operated by the Passaic County Department of Parks and Recreation, but what makes it one of the most active historic sites in New Jersey is the work of a loyal volunteer army. The two-story brick Georgian mansion hosts a full calendar of events, including many colonial-life demonstrations and Continental army reenactments and encampments. Reenactors like Paul Doll, a member of two Continental army units, show up in authentic-looking uniforms and demonstrate the use of period weapons.

Inside, there are a number of paintings and portraits of Washington, including a reproduction of the Gilbert Stewart portrait that is familiar to anyone who has ever spent a U.S. dollar bill.

The house is filled with period furniture, but the only thing there Washington ever actually used is a set of pewter plates in the dining room.

The Schuyler-Colfax House
Hamburg Turnpike
(973) 694-7192
HOURS: Friday and Saturday, 1 P.M. to 5 P.M.

On a busy stretch of the Hamburg Turnpike, sandwiched between a used-car lot and a new-car dealership, is the Schuyler-Colfax House. Washington stayed here July 11–14, 1777, according to the research of the D.A.R.'s Susan Deckert of Hamilton.

The house was built in 1695 by Arent Schuyler, a mining baron who had a number of substantial properties throughout New Jersey. At the time of the Revolution, the house was still in the family—which included young, pretty (and rich) Hester Schuyler. During Washington's stay here, Capt. William Colfax, second in command of Washington's Life Guard, began to court Miss Schuyler. He later married her.

General and Mrs. Washington visited the house a few years later for the christening of one of the Colfaxes' sons, George Washington Colfax. Another son, Schuyler Colfax, was vice president of the United States under Ulysses S. Grant.

The house today is a museum owned by the town.

Van Saun House (Lafayette Headquarters)
23 Laauwe Avenue
(Private)

The Marquis de Lafayette stayed in this house while Washington was at the Dey Mansion in July 1780. In October and November, Lafayette made his headquarters in the Ryerson House, which stood in what is now Goffle Brook Park in Hawthorne. That house was in the vicinity of what today is Goffle Road and Diamond Bridge Avenue.

New Jersey Brigade Encampment Site
Vicinity of Fairfield and Two Bridges Roads

The New Jersey Brigade camped in this area, including what today is Pequannock River Park, during the Preakness encampments while Washington was headquartered at the Dey Mansion.

West Milford

Long Pond Iron Works
Greenwood Lake Turnpike
(973) 839-0128
HOURS: Unavailable.

This deserted village is undergoing extensive renovation by a group called the Friends of the Long Pond Iron Works. The furnace here had its iron-making heyday in the mid-1800s, but during the Revolution it was a fairly significant iron producer for the Continental army. The site today has the ruins of a number of fieldstone houses and other structures in a very beautiful, wooded setting. The remains of the village on the road may be opened some day as a working museum.

West Paterson

Preakness Encampment and Lookout Site
Rifle Camp Road and Old Rifle Camp Road at Route 46

Maj. James Parr commanded a rifle unit which camped here while Washington was in Wayne. The main campsite was at the present-day junction of Rifle Camp Road and Route 46.

Up the hill in Great Notch, in what today is Rifle Camp Park, was a lookout site. The ridge offers imposing views of the Hackensack and Passaic River Valleys.

There was also a fire beacon on this hill, as well as a signal cannon—all part of Lord Stirling's beacon-alarm system, which stretched throughout the Watchung Mountains into the New Jersey Highlands.

The Shore Counties

MONMOUTH, ATLANTIC, OCEAN, AND CAPE MAY

On June 29, 1776, an American brig carrying gunpowder and weapons was run aground off Cape May by a British warship. As the captain and crew worked frantically to unload the precious cargo, British troops boarded the ship. In the fighting and explosion that followed, an American named Richard Wickes was killed, the first to die on New Jersey soil.

On the same day, a massive British force landed on Sandy Hook and took control of that strategic spot. The British held it for the next five years.

At about the same time, two companies of Burlington County militia were sent to Monmouth County to round up suspected Loyalist and Tory spies.

The war at the shore was on.

Monmouth County, with its rich farmlands to the west and access to the ocean to the east, had everything an invading army could ask for. Its residents were constantly under attack—their food bins pillaged, their livestock stolen, and their homes plundered. Tory bandits became such a problem that Washington had to appoint a local—Gen. David Forman—to stamp them out.

On the other side, Congress-backed American pirates—who went by the more socially acceptable name of "privateers"—caused so much trouble that the British sent a special force to stamp them out.

The shore counties were in action throughout the Revolution: the biggest battle of the war was fought near Monmouth Court House, the Sandy

Hook Lighthouse was under constant siege, American privateers engaged the British almost weekly in offshore skirmishes.

Add to this a few legends (like Molly Pitcher), a few heroes (like Capt. Joshua Huddy), and a few villains (like Gen. Charles Lee) and you'll find as colorful a Revolutionary War history as anywhere.

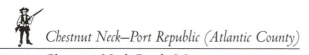

Chestnut Neck–Port Republic (Atlantic County)

Chestnut Neck Battle Monument
Routes 9 and 575
(south of Exit 48 on the Garden State Parkway)

During the war, Congress commissioned about four hundred fifty sea captains, known as privateers, to go out and pirate British shipping. A great many of these captains operated in the Ocean and Atlantic County region, especially out of the Mullica River. This area was perfect for maritime guerrilla warfare for a number of reasons. First, there were established boat-building operations in the area. Second, the British had strongholds in New York and Philadelphia for much of the war, and the New Jersey shipping lanes were filled with ships flying the Union Jack. Third, the tidewater rivers, coves, and inlets in the area were hard for warships to navigate, so that the privateers had hideout protection from the British navy.

The action between these privateers and the British fleet is an underreported aspect of the Revolutionary War in New Jersey. Of the 787 conflicts listed on the *Battles and Skirmishes of the American Revolution* map, roughly one-third were naval confrontations.

The New Jersey privateers operated between the New York and Delaware bays—off Sandy Hook and Staten Island and throughout the New Jersey barrier islands all the way down to Cape May. Many were driven by patriotism, all were driven by profit. In fact, what they got from Congress was a license to steal. So brazen were these privateer-profiteers, that they regularly advertised auctions for stolen goods in the newspaper.

Here is an example, taken from William McMahon's *South Jersey Towns: History and Legend* (see the Research chapter), of a typical ad from the *Pennsylvania Packet*, September 3, 1778:

> By way of Public Vendue on Monday the 14th ... at the Forks of Little Egg-Harbor and Chestnut Neck, New Jersey. A very valuable Cargo of the Ship "VENUS" ... lately captured and brought there by Capt. David Stevens, consisting of fine coarse broadclothes, fine and coarse

linens, . . . Silks, Sattens, Silk and threat stockings, Men and Wom-
ens Shoes, a great variety of Medicines, etc. The vendue to begin at
10 o'clock in the forenoon and to continue until the whole is sold.

Gen. Henry Clinton, the British commander in chief, wanted the
"rebel pirates" rooted out and selected Capt. Patrick Ferguson, a young gun
inventor who in September 1777, before the Battle of Brandywine, had had
a chance to assassinate Washington from a distance. Ferguson wrote later
that he had not fired because "it was not pleasant to fire at the back of an
unoffending individual who was acquitting himself very coolly of his duty,
so I let him alone."

In charge of a three-hundred-man British foot regiment and another one
hundred New Jersey Loyalists during his attack on the coast, Ferguson
himself "very coolly" took care of business. During a three-week period in
October 1778, he did extensive damage in the area.

The first incident took place at Chestnut Neck on October 6, 1778.
Although Ferguson and his men put ashore under fire from local militia, the
professional British soldiers soon drove the locals back. They burned ten ships,
the shipyard, and the mill; destroyed a saltworks; and set fire to the village
of Chestnut Neck before returning to their ships.

Despite this damage, the people of Chestnut Neck and the Mullica River
privateers were back in business as soon as the British left, and they continued
throughout the war.

Although it stands fifty feet tall and is topped by a colonial privateer,
the Chestnut Neck Battle Monument is one of the most obscure major Revolutionary War sites in New Jersey. The battle shows up in very few histories of the Revolution and most Jerseyans have never heard of it.

This particularly irks Port Republic Mayor Gary Giberson, whose
family in the town dates back to the war. "The actions of these privateers
won the war," he said. "They made it too costly for the British to get
supplies. . . . It made the war effort too expensive for the British."

At this writing, Giberson is leading an effort to build a privateers' museum
on town land directly across Route 9 from the monument.

Captain Micajah Smith House (The Franklin Inn)
Mill Street (just west of Main Street)
(Private)

A historical marker stands in front of the home of Micajah Smith, a privateer and mill owner who supplied wood to the shipbuilding industry on

MARK DI IONNO

The Privateer Cemetery, Port Republic

Nacote Creek (next to the house). Many of the privateer ships were built on the Nacote, which dumps out into the Mullica River. In the burning of Chestnut Neck, innkeeper Daniel Mathis's place was torched. He bought Smith's house and called it the Franklin Inn.

Smith's Meeting House and Blackman's Cemetery
Near corner of English Creek Road, Port Republic Road
(Route 575), and Indian Cabin Road

Take Main Street west from the Franklin Inn site and you will see a Revolutionary War cemetery about a quarter of a mile on the left. Micajah Smith and fellow privateer Capt. John Van Sant are buried here, along with a number of Revolutionary War soldiers.

Colts Neck (Monmouth County)

Joshua Huddy Monument
Colts Neck Town Hall
Cedar Drive

Joshua Huddy, an aggressive commander of the New Jersey militia in Central Monmouth County, was the target of a number of British and

Loyalist raids. Captured twice, he escaped once but was hanged at Highlands. The British commander in chief, Gen. Henry Clinton, described this incident as an "act of barbarity" in a letter of explanation to Washington.

Huddy, who owned an inn and lived along Colts Neck Road (Route 537), was first captured by a band of Loyalists led by a mixed-race escaped slave named Titus, who was also known as Colonel Tye. According to *The WPA Guide to 1930s New Jersey* (see the Research chapter), Huddy's home was "attacked by Colonel Tye and some 60 followers. . . . Huddy and a young Negro servant girl, the only occupants of the house, put up a strong defense for hours. When attackers set fire to the house, Huddy surrendered. The girl escaped. Crossing Shrewsbury River with his captors Huddy jumped overboard and won freedom. Colonial militia pursued the raiders and killed six; Tye died later of a wound."

Huddy didn't fare as well in the second incident. On March 24, 1782, a group of Loyalists known as "Refugees" attacked the blockhouse at Toms River, where Huddy and his men were stationed. The Patriots fought until they ran out of gunpowder, then surrendered. Huddy was captured and taken to a British prison ship in New York. British authorities released him to the Loyalists, believing that he would be exchanged for Loyalist prisoners. Instead, the Loyalist contingent, led by Capt. Richard Lippincott, summarily hanged Huddy (see the Highlands section of this chapter) in retaliation for the killing of Loyalist Philip White. (Some accounts say Huddy may have killed White, but according to Dennis Ryan's *Chronology of the American Revolution* [see the Research chapter], White was not killed until six days after Huddy was taken into custody.) Huddy was buried at Tennent Church (see the Manalapan section of this chapter).

The incident reverberated throughout the colonies and to the top of the military chain of command. Washington wrote Gen. Henry Clinton, the British commander in chief, and demanded that the responsible officer be handed over. Clinton was appalled, but he could not produce the guilty party. Washington lost patience and had Lippincott arrested. Lippincott's trial defense was that he was simply following orders, and he was acquitted. Washington held a council of war on the matter, and it was decided that a British prisoner, picked by lottery, should be executed in retaliation. Capt. Charles Asgill, who had been captured at Yorktown, was the unlucky loser. Washington, however—even though he did not want Huddy's death to go unpunished—was against the capital punishment of an innocent man.

He found a suitable political escape from this dilemma when Asgill's mother wrote an impassioned plea to the French for his release. The French formally asked Washington to release Asgill and Washington passed the plea on to Congress. Congress voted to let Asgill go free, to Washington's relief.

The entire incident illustrates the intense civil war within the war between England and the colonies. Huddy and Lippincott were neighbors, and some say even friends, before they became divided by politics. White, a Monmouth County Loyalist, was killed as he tried to escape after killing the son of a Monmouth militiaman. Also, the incident occurred five months after the British surrendered at Yorktown. Even though the war was effectively over, this civil war continued in New Jersey—mostly in Monmouth County—until Governor William Livingston ordered an end to all hostilities on April 14, 1783.

The Colts Neck Inn
Corner of Colts Neck Road (Route 537) and Route 34

An enduring legend in the area says Joshua Huddy was the proprietor of this inn, but there is no evidence to prove it. There is also no evidence that Washington ever stayed here. The inn, built in 1717, is on the road between Freehold and Red Bank, and it is almost certain that the British marched past it while retreating from Monmouth.

Michael Field Memorial Park
North end of Heyer's Mill Road
Michael Field Grave Site

Michael Field was just an ordinary member of the New Jersey militia, no different from thousands of other soldiers who died in the Revolution. The Somerset County lad died from wounds received in either the Battle of Monmouth or some outlying skirmish connected with the main event.

Like almost all soldiers of the day, he was buried on the spot. Unlike most of the soldiers of the day, his grave was marked, presumably by his family—first with a tombstone, and later with a wrought-iron fence. When Field died, his final resting place was all woods. Later it became a farmer's field, and Michael Field's grave site became a local oddity—a wrought-iron-fenced grave in the middle of a plowed field.

Grave Site of Private Michael Field

When the town wanted to build a veterans' memorial park, Field's grave gave them a head start. The local oddity became the centerpiece of the little park, which is now wooded again.

Englishtown (Monmouth County)

General David Forman House
Amberly Drive (in Covered Bridge condominium complex
    off Route 9)
(Private)

When Washington wanted the Tory raids in Monmouth County to come to an end, he turned to David Forman, then a colonel in his army. Forman hunted down and hanged the raiders with such quickness and force that he soon earned the nickname "Black David."

The Forman house is not marked and is not on anybody's historic homes list. The small yellow house is behind the condo association's clubhouse, surrounded by the pool, tennis, and bocce courts. It is used for storage, and the condo association has no plans to open it to the public.

General David Forman House

The Village Inn
Corner of Main and Water Streets
HOURS: By appointment.

The plaque at this inn says that Gen. Charles Lee's court-martial was held here after the Battle of Monmouth, but in fact it was held over a six-week period, beginning in New Brunswick and ending in Paramus.

There is also a local legend that Washington drew up the three charges for court-martial against Lee here, but that is also not true.

If anything, what happened at the Village Inn was this: after the Battle of Monmouth, Lee came here and wrote an ill-conceived letter to Washington. He called Washington's berating of him in the field at Monmouth a "cruel injustice" and demanded "some reparation for the injury committed."

Washington, who may have also been at the inn, offered him an official hearing. Lee in turn demanded an immediate full court-martial, misguidedly thinking that the trial would embarrass Washington. Washington had him placed under arrest immediately and the trial began within days. Lee was found guilty of all three charges: (1) disobeying orders, (2) misbehavior before the enemy (including shameful retreat), and (3) disrespecting the commander in chief.

The Village Inn is operated by the Battleground Historical Society. There are no regular hours. Those interested in seeing the inn can write the group at P.O. Box 161, Tennent, N.J. 07763.

Freehold (Monmouth County)

Monmouth County Historical Association
70 Court Street
(723) 462-1466
HOURS: Tuesday through Saturday, 10 A.M. to 4 P.M.; Sunday 1 P.M.
to 4 P.M. The library is open Wednesday through Saturday,
10 A.M. to 4 P.M.

The museum at the historical association has a good number of Monmouth battlefield artifacts, including a very rare Continental army linen knapsack and red-letter cartridge belt, three muskets, a tobacco box, musket balls and grapeshot, and socks.

MARK DI IONNO

Molly Pitcher Depiction on Monmouth Battle Monument

In the main hall hangs a seven-by-five-foot copy of *Washington at the Battle of Monmouth*, the famous painting by Emanuel Leutze. The 1857 original, about fourteen feet long, hangs in the Berkeley Art Gallery in California.

Leutze made a second copy of the painting after the first was criticized for portraying Washington as too angry. The paintings are "virtually identical except for Washington's face," said Bernadette Rogoff, the curator at the historical association. "People didn't accept seeing Washington as a human. In our painting, he has a very stoic expression on his face."

Across the street from the museum is the imposing Monmouth Battle Monument, dedicated in 1884. The ninety-four-foot-high memorial is topped by a Continental soldier. Copper relief panels near the base depict characters and scenes connected with the battle: *Molly Pitcher, Wayne's Charge, Washington Takes Charge, Washington's Council at Hopewell.*

Monmouth County Hall of Records
Corner of Main and Court Streets

This is the site of the courthouse where the British left forty-five injured prisoners in a makeshift sick bay before vacating the area.

St. Peter's Episcopal Church
33 Throckmorton Street

One of the oldest continually used churches in New Jersey, St. Peter's served both sides during the war. The British used it as a hospital during and after the Battle of Monmouth, and the Americans used it as a barracks and an ammunition depot.

The Covenhoven House
150 West Main Street
(732) 462-1466
HOURS: Tuesday, Thursday, and Sunday, 1 P.M. to 4 P.M.; Saturday, 10 A.M. to 4 P.M. May through September. Closed on major holidays.

The house was owned by William and Libertje Covenhoven at the time of the Revolution. In the days leading up to the Monmouth battle, when the British commander in chief, Gen. Henry Clinton, used it as his headquarters, William Covenhoven wasn't at the house. It is said that Clinton and his officers forced Mrs. Covenhoven to sleep in an outdoor shed while they made themselves at home. This house is owned and operated by the Monmouth County Historical Association.

MARK DI IONNO

The Covenhoven House, Clinton's Headquarters

Highlands (Monmouth County)

Captain Joshua Huddy Monument
Waterwitch Avenue and Bayside Drive

A Sons of the American Revolution monument marks the spot where Capt. Joshua Huddy, a leading officer in the New Jersey militia, was hanged on April 12, 1782, by Loyalists under the command of Capt. Richard Lippincott.

The Huddy incident demonstrates the intense civil-war nature of the Revolution. The Loyalists accused Huddy of killing Philip White, one of their own, and wanted Huddy's death to serve as a warning to all Patriots. After Huddy was hanged, Lippincott hung a sign on him that said: "We, the Refugees, having long with the grief beheld the cruel murders of our brethren . . . [and] determined not to suffer without taking vengeance . . . and thus begin, having made Captain Huddy as the first object to present to your view; and we further determine to hang man for man while there is a Refugee existing. . . . Up goes Huddy for Philip White."

Holmdel (Monmouth County)

Site of the "Hornet's Nest"
Long Bridge Road and East Main Street

Here at the Smock farmhouse was a center of rebel activity that has come to be known as the "Hornet's Nest." This area on the Holmdel-Marlboro border, known as Pleasant Valley, was the site of three significant skirmishes. One occurred on the same day as the Monmouth battle. Another came nearly three years later when one thousand Tories under the leadership of Cortlandt Skinner raided the area. They were driven away by angry residents reinforced by the militia.

Holmes-Hendrickson House
62 Longstreet Road (next to Longstreet County Park)
(732) 462-1466
HOURS: Tuesday, Thursday, and Sunday, 1 P.M. to 4 P.M.;
         Saturday, 10 A.M. to 4 P.M. May through September.
         Closed on major holidays.

The third major skirmish in Pleasant Valley happened at this house, which today is operated by the Monmouth County Historical Association.

Garrett Hendrickson was a first lieutenant in the county militia who got hit by a musket ball and lost the use of his right arm in 1780. On the night of February 8, 1782, forty Loyalists landed at Sandy Hook with the intention of pillaging Pleasant Valley. They attacked Hendrickson's house and captured him along with other militiamen. But Garrett's son, Hendrick Hendrickson, escaped and sounded the nearby general alarm. The militia responded and, once again, drove the invaders away.

Little Egg Harbor (Ocean County)

Pulaski Monument
South Pulaski Boulevard and Kosciusko Way
(Near the site of the Little Egg Harbor Massacre)

The number of inlets, coves, bays, harbors, and rivers along the Ocean and Atlantic County coastline made it a perfect area for New Jersey privateers to harass British shipping. (See the Chestnut Neck–Port Republic section of this chapter.)

On his mission to stamp out the privateers, Capt. Patrick Ferguson and a force of two hundred fifty men landed at Osborn Island and attacked an American outpost under the command of Count Casimir Pulaski. Pulaski had been dispatched by Washington to try to repel Ferguson's attacks on the shipyards and villages in the area.

Pulaski had his headquarters in the old Willets-Andrews farmhouse north of Osborn Island in what today is Little Egg Harbor Township. The farmhouse burned down in the 1930s, but its foundation remains on the site, a vacant lot on Hollybrook Drive near the intersection with Cedarbrook, just south of the Atlantis Country Club off Radio Road.

If you continue south on Radio Road, the Pulaski Monument is off to the left. Turn left where Kadlubeck Way intersects with Radio Road, and the monument is on a knoll to your left.

The little monument, erected by the Sons of Cincinnati in 1894, is on the site of a house where two hundred fifty British soldiers surprised about forty Americans in a Pulaski outpost in the early morning of October 15, 1778. After bayoneting some of the sleeping men, the British burned down the house. Different accounts give different numbers of the dead, but Pulaski himself reported twenty-five. Most were buried on the spot.

Both sites were saved from development by the Affair at Egg Harbor Society, which hopes to put a monument at the Pulaski headquarters site someday.

 Manalapan (Monmouth County)

Monmouth Battlefield State Park
347 Freehold Road (Route 33)
(732) 462-9616
HOURS: The Visitors' Center is open every day from 9 A.M.
        to 4 P.M. Outdoor areas of the park are open from
        dawn to dusk.

On a brutally hot day in the fields around the tiny Central Jersey village of Monmouth Court House, the biggest, longest battle of the Revolution began with a shot before dawn and ended with the British sneaking away after dark. It was a battle that gave birth to an American heroine, solidified Washington's reputation as a field leader, and raised the status of the American army from amateur to professional.

It was a battle that, in truth, covered about a fifteen-mile span. The main site, or "killing fields," as state historian Garry Wheeler Stone likes to say, was the soft hills and meadows between Tennent and what today is Freehold. But there were many skirmishes throughout Monmouth County between New Jersey militia and the British regulars who were protecting their twelve-mile, fifteen-hundred-wagon supply train, which was wending its way toward Sandy Hook.

The stage for the Battle of Monmouth was set when the British evacuated Philadelphia in mid-June 1778, marching northeast across Burlington County into western Monmouth on their way to Sandy Hook, where they would ship out to New York. On the move here was the main British army: about seventeen thousand men and fifteen hundred wagons of artillery and supplies.

Washington, in Valley Forge, was determined not to let the British move through New Jersey unscathed. He put his army of thirteen thousand men in pursuit, crossing the Delaware at Lambertville.

In the days leading up to the battle, the weather was more like a Jersey August than June: it was hot and thickly humid. The British were carrying full packs over soft, sandy roads, and the march took a toll. A good number died of heatstroke as Clinton led them through the villages and farmlands of Burlington.

The Continental army was disorganized in its pursuit, but the slow-moving supply train of the British allowed Washington to stay within striking distance.

On June 28, 1778, the British began moving out at 4 A.M. Gen. Charles Lee, back in action after being captured by the British (see the Somerset County chapter), advanced with his force of five thousand men on the British rear guard. The idea was to encircle and engage the rear guard, but soon Lee realized that a full half of the British army was returning for a fight. Lee's troops fell back in a panicked retreat instead of standing and fighting to give the eight thousand men under Washington a chance to enter the battle and establish a strong position. At this point Washington intercepted Lee and demanded that he stand and fight. When Lee balked, Washington took charge and led a counterattack.

The encounter was memorialized in the Emanuel Leutze painting seventy years later. Washington apparently unleashed years of pent-up anger at his longtime antagonist, calling him a "damned poltroon" and challenging his courage and loyalty, and ordered him to the rear. Gen. Charles Scott, a witness to the incident, said Washington "swore . . . till the leaves shook on the trees."

Washington rode through the lines, rallying the men, and the rest is history: the longest battle of the Revolution and the one that involved the most men. The British held a position on the east side of the park near the hedgerow, while the Americans took the high ground in the northwest corner. With available heavy artillery about even, the two sides pounded away at each other throughout the miserably hot day.

Gen. Nathaniel Greene was able to bring up four guns on the left flank of the British in late afternoon, and the exhausted redcoats retreated from the site.

After dark, as Washington planned a second attack for the next morning, the British headed off toward Sandy Hook, anxious to get out of New Jersey.

Historians like to say Monmouth was the last major battle in the north, but to say that is to diminish the Battle of Springfield (see the Union County chapter).

However, the battle marked the first time the Americans had beaten the British in the open field. It was a battle in which Washington proved himself as a field marshal and in which the American troops, thanks to the training of Baron Frederick William von Steuben, proved themselves as a well-disciplined fighting force.

There is no better illustration of this than the death of Lt. Henry Monckton, who was in command of the redcoat elite troops. Three times they charged an American line commanded by "Mad" Anthony Wayne. Each time, Wayne had his men stand their ground. The last time, he let the British advance so close that he and Monckton could hear one another's orders.

"Forward to the charge, my brave grenadiers," Monckton is said to have ordered as he led a full-speed charge.

"Steady . . . steady," Wayne told his troops. "Wait for the word, then pick out the kingbirds."

When the British came within forty yards, Wayne ordered his troops to fire. The British charge disintegrated into a heap of falling men, one of whom was Monckton. He was so close that some of the Americans went out and seized his sword and colors as trophies of war.

Then, of course, there is the story of Molly Pitcher, who shows up in every grammar-school history book—not to mention the New Jersey Turnpike rest stop that is named after her. Molly Ludwig Hays was married to a gunner named John Hays. She spent most of the day fetching water for the troops. But legend has it that when her husband was hit, she replaced him on the gun.

She has been memorialized by a Molly Pitcher marker on Route 522 (now gone) and a Molly Pitcher well on the battlefield, both claiming to mark the spot where she made her legend. In fact, it all happened in neither place. According to Stone, the real spot is toward the northernmost corner of the park, about two thousand feet northeast of the Conover-Perrine House (c. 1832).

"She was on the north end of the American lines," he said. "Between there and the Old Tennent Church was a deep ravine with a fresh spring in it. That's where it all happened."

Also in error was a road marker on Route 522 near the Englishtown-Manalapan border that marked the site of the Washington-Lee dustup. In fact, the encounter took place about a mile and a quarter east, in a field just opposite where Route 522 meets Ilene Way.

Monmouth Battlefield State Park is one of the state's best Revolutionary War stops. The park area remained undeveloped for the two centuries between the battle and the state's taking it over. In the last few years, nearly a million dollars has been made available to do a historical restoration of the vegetation. "We want to re-create the original woodlands," said Stone of the twenty-five-hundred acre battlefield.

In the visitors' center museum are exhibits on weapons and uniforms, a hanging copy of the New Jersey *Battles and Skirmishes* map, an electric map of the battle, and a diorama of the death of Monckton.

Matawan (Monmouth County)

Philip Freneau Grave Site
112 Poet Drive

Philip Freneau led a fascinating life. Born in Freehold, he was educated at Princeton, where he was a friend of James Madison. He was a poet of great literary merit and used his talent to further the rebel cause. He cowrote *The Rising Glory of America* early in the war and published a number of satires aimed at the British.

He also was a privateer captain who, when captured, suffered at the hands of the British and had to be transferred to a hospital ship. After the war, he returned to the sea and wrote detailed poems based on his experience of the beauty and dangers of the ocean. He began Monmouth County's first newspaper, and was cited by Jefferson for his strong First Amendment views.

On December 19, 1832, the eighty-year-old Freneau, who survived war-time imprisonment as well as shipwrecks and hurricanes, died after getting lost in a blizzard while walking home from the local general store. His grave is well marked by a white obelisk near this spot.

Burrowes Mansion
94 Main Street
(732) 566-5605
HOURS: First and third Sunday of each month, 2 P.M. to 4 P.M.

It is said that the first group of New Jersey militiamen were organized on the front lawn of the Burrowes Mansion by John Burrowes Jr., and that he drilled the men in the back yard. John Burrowes Sr., a grain merchant, supplied the Continental army with corn.

A group of Loyalists from Staten Island attacked the house in an effort to capture Burrowes Jr., but he escaped just before they arrived. His wife refused to disclose his whereabouts and was slashed by a sword. She later died of the wound.

Failing to find their quarry, the Loyalists took John Burrowes Sr. off with a number of other prominent residents of the town but later let them return safely.

 *Middletown (Monmouth County)*

Marlpit Hall
137 Kings Highway
(732) 462-1466
HOURS: Unavailable.

At the time of Revolution, Marlpit Hall was owned by the prosperous Taylor family. The Taylors had prospered economically and politically under British rule, and when war was imminent they chose to stay loyal to the crown.

The patriarch of the family was Edward Taylor, a miller. He was the largest landowner in Middletown, with twelve hundred acres, and was a political officeholder similar to a mayor. His son, George, was a Loyalist colonel.

Edward Taylor was suspected of cooperating with the British and was placed under house arrest until war's end. When the war was over, this prominent family had lost its wealth and social position. The house is owned and operated by the Monmouth County Historical Association.

Rumson (Monmouth County)

Joshua Huddy Monument
Rumson Road (on west side of the Shrewsbury River Bridge)

Near the west side of the bridge is a small grassy area where there stands another monument to Huddy. A few years before he was captured and hanged by Tory "Refugees," he was taken into custody at his tavern in Colts Neck. As the raiders transported him to Sandy Hook by boat, Huddy escaped by jumping into the Shrewsbury River at this site. The monument plaque tells the story.

Sandy Hook (Monmouth County)

The Lighthouse
(closed to public)

During the Revolution the lighthouse was an eighty-five-foot pawn in the battle over the shipping lanes. Patriots who had wanted the lighthouse built in 1764 now wanted it destroyed in hopes of sending a few British warships and supply ships into the shoals.

According to David C. Munn's *Battles and Skirmishes of the American Revolution*, there were eighteen incidents at Sandy Hook, many near or around the lighthouse.

On June 21, 1776, three hundred Americans attacked the British outpost at the lighthouse but were driven back. On July 3, five hundred tried again. On March 1, 1777, two hundred fifty made a run at the lighthouse, but they were repelled by shelling from the British warship *Syren.* The lighthouse survived, and today it is the oldest working lighthouse in the nation.

There were also a number of naval skirmishes in the waters off Sandy Hook. The chief American protagonist was New Jerseyan Adam Hyler, a whaleboat captain who captured or destroyed a significant number of British and Tory boats in the shoals on the Hook.

Fighting went on with some regularity around Sandy Hook for most of the war. The first skirmish was in January 1776, the last in July 1782.

The Halyburton Monument

Two miles north of the Spermaceti Cove visitors' center on the main park road is a monument to the disastrous Halyburton expedition in December 1783.

First Lieutenant Hamilton Douglas Halyburton, an officer aboard the British frigate *Assistance*, left the ship with thirteen men to round up deserters in the Sandy Hook area. The rowboat capsized in a blizzard and all of the men either drowned or froze to death near Horseshoe Cove.

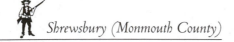

Shrewsbury (Monmouth County)

The Allen House

400 Sycamore Avenue (at Route 35)
(732) 462-1466
HOURS: Tuesday, Thursday, and Sunday, 1 P.M. to 4 P.M.;
　　　　Saturday, 10 A.M. to 4 P.M. May through September.
　　　　Closed on major holidays.

There were fourteen documented skirmishes in Shrewsbury and Shrewsbury Township, where the war between neighbors in Monmouth County was most intense. The first took place in 1775, the last six years later. The Allen House, a tavern at the time, was a hotbed of revolutionary activity. In the summer of 1775 it was attacked by a Loyalist patrol led by Joseph Price, who was married to a former owner of the tavern. Price and his men surprised a group of Continental army soldiers stationed there and bayoneted three rebels. The house today is owned and operated by the Monmouth County Historical Association.

Across the street from the Allen House are the Old Quaker Meeting House and the Episcopal Church, both of which were there during the Revolution. The church took a musket ball in the steeple crown during one of the skirmishes. The ball is displayed in an exhibit case in the church foyer.

Tennent (Monmouth County)

Old Tennent Church

445 Tennent Road (Monmouth Route 3)
(732) 446-6299

From the hilltop where this church sits, Washington watched parts of the battle at Monmouth. At the front door, he held an impromptu war council. In the churchyard are buried the Monmouth County Revolutionary War hero Joshua Huddy and the British lieutenant colonel Henry Monckton, along with about a hundred other veterans of the conflict. From the steeple, American officers had a bird's-eye view of the day-long battle, and sent messengers with reports of British troop movement into the field. In the days after the battle, the church served as a hospital for wounded Americans.

But the most important part this Presbyterian Church played in the Revolution came in the years before the first shot was ever fired. In fact, the role of all Calvinist churches in the colonies has been vastly underestimated, according to the current Tennent pastor, the Reverend Dr. Hugh MacKenzie.

Old Tennent Church

"At that time in history, wherever Calvinists went, revolution followed," said MacKenzie. "We didn't see government and church as two separate spheres. If God is sovereign, he is sovereign over all culture, including government. We took democracy seriously because it was part of the religion. We preached rights, rights, rights. There are a number of Calvinist doctrines that have language very similar to the Declaration of Independence and the Constitution."

During a period called the Great Awakening in the 1730s, a good number of Presbyterian ministers spent time preaching throughout the colonies. MacKenzie said Tennent's church was a major stop, "one of the centers of Calvinist preaching."

A network of pastors was developing, among them Aaron Burr Sr. and William Tennent Jr. They formed "committees of correspondence" throughout the colonies.

"These were the first people who developed a network of communication among the colonies," said MacKenzie. "This was the precursor to committees of government that led to the Revolution."

Joshua Huddy Park, Toms River

Toms River (Ocean County)

Joshua Huddy Park
East Water Street

Toms River was the site of the one of the most important saltworks in the colonies. The salt, derived from sea water, was used in preserving food and making gunpowder.

On Christmas night 1777, Col. John Morris, a Tory, tried to destroy the saltworks but was driven away. In 1778 the British stepped up their saltworks-destroying mission with a special eye on Toms River. One hundred thirty-five men attacked Toms River on April 15 and destroyed the plant. The saltworks was quickly rebuilt, and a blockhouse was constructed at the spot where the Toms River widens, to protect the saltworks. It was at this fort on March 24, 1782, that Capt. Joshua Huddy was captured after his garrison of twenty-five men surrendered to a much larger force of Loyalist "Refugees." Huddy was taken to New York. He was later hanged at Highlands in one of the most controversial events of the war (see the Colts Neck and Highlands sections of this chapter).

Near the site of the old blockhouse is a replica with a large plaque that tells the story.

Somerset County

Washington marched through Somerset County on his way to Morristown after his victories at Trenton and Princeton, and the French army marched through on its way to Yorktown.

But Somerset County was much more than just a transportation corridor. It was a place hotly contested by both sides, the buffer zone between the Americans in the Watchungs and the British in New Brunswick. The area along the Raritan River was especially hot. It was the scene of a number of significant battles and events, and the people who lived in it found themselves playing host alternately to American and British troops.

No county has a greater collection of Revolutionary War characters than Somerset: John Honeyman and Abraham Staats, the spies; the daring British raider John Simcoe; the Anglophile arch-Patriot Lord Stirling; the brilliant but self-destructive Gen. Charles Lee—an opportunistic Britisher-turned-American who let his ambition destroy him; the eighty-year-old rabble-rouser Hendrick Fisher; and Washington's rotund big-gun expert, Gen. Henry Knox. There is even a famous ghost.

Yes, Somerset is a Revolutionary War storyteller's dream. Here are most of the stories.

Basking Ridge

Widow White's Tavern Site
Corner of South Finley Avenue and Colonial Drive
As Washington retreated across New Jersey in November and December 1776,

he ordered Gen. Charles Lee to bring his force of seven thousand men down from New York State to meet him near the Delaware.

Lee, a British-born and -trained military man, decided instead to go to Morristown "in the hopes . . . to reconquer the Jerseys."

Washington fumed, while Lee outright disobeyed his orders.

This incident epitomized the relationship between Washington and Lee, who was essentially his third in command. Lee saw himself as better equipped—militarily and intellectually—to lead the Americans against his motherland. He was stubborn and uncooperative and his actions on many occasions were often in direct conflict with Washington's wishes. The only explanation is that Lee, the English professional soldier, was hoping that the green Yankee Washington would fail and that Congress would turn to him to rescue the cause.

Lee was also despised by the British command, who saw him as a deserter and a traitor. When Gen. Charles Cornwallis heard that Lee was in New Jersey, he made up his mind to capture him and take him to Gen. William Howe.

Cornwallis dispatched Lt. Col. William Harcourt and a squad of twenty-five horsemen to get Lee. The squad belonged to the Seventeenth Light Dragoons, which Lee had once commanded. British Loyalists helped the dragoons look for him. The British then intercepted an American messenger, who, faced with death, disclosed Lee's location.

In the early morning of Friday, December 13, 1776, while Washington's men were huddled against the elements on the other side of the Delaware, General Lee was sleeping soundly in the tavern of the widow White.

The British squad surrounded the house in the dark and, at daybreak, surprised Lee's guards. Hearing the commotion, Lee tried to hide in the house, but when Harcourt announced that he would burn it down Lee surrendered in his nightshirt and slippers. It is said that the British cut off his ponytail and tied him to the saddle of a horse for the ride to New Brunswick.

Gen. John Sullivan, second in command of Lee's troops, then took the army to join Washington in time for the Christmas attack on Trenton.

The tavern was demolished just before World War II. At one point it had been renamed Lee Lodge.

Basking Ridge Presbyterian Church
1 East Oak Street
(908) 766-1616

It is believed that this church, with its famous six-hundred-year-old oak tree, was a favorite resting stop for Washington and his officers and that the ladies of the church delighted in serving Washington refreshments. Under the oak tree, Washington and the Marquis de Lafayette once had a picnic.

At least thirty-five former Revolutionary War soldiers are buried in the church cemetery. There is also an enduring legend that Betsy Ross is buried in the churchyard.

According to Morristown National Historical Park historian Eric Olsen, the Jockey Hollow camp hospital was nearby, in a ravine by the stream that parallels North Finley Avenue.

Lord Stirling Estate Site
Lord Stirling Road and South Maple Avenue

Lord Stirling (William Alexander) was one of the most colorful characters of the Revolution. Born into a wealthy family, he nonetheless loved soldiering. He was an officer in the French and Indian Wars, and he served in the Revolution from the beginning of the war until his death on January 15, 1783. His father was a Scottish expatriate lawyer and his mother was the widow of a wealthy merchant. Nevertheless, during a stay in England in the late 1750s he attempted to lay claim to the title of Earl of Stirling. While he was never granted the title, he took to calling himself Lord Stirling and was widely known by that name. Even Washington is reported to have addressed him as "My Lord," although it is not known whether the general may just have been indulging his friend's quirkiness.

Lord Stirling had a six-hundred-acre estate in the area that today is Lord Stirling County Park and the southwest end of the Great Swamp National Wildlife Refuge. The main house burned down in the 1920s. By many accounts, Lord Stirling lived like a king and his estate was unequaled in the colonies. During the war he was alternately seen as a brilliant military officer and a bumbling incompetent. His most glorious moment may have been at the Battle of Ash Swamp (see the Union County chapter), where his men held fast against a superior British force.

There were two great ironies in his life. First, although he was an ardent Patriot he clung to a title and a lifestyle of privilege. Second, after fighting in at least five major engagements and even being captured—at the Battle of Long Island—he died of gout at age fifty-six.

The historical marker for the site is on Lord Stirling Road.

Washington's Route Marker
Corner of North Maple and Madisonville Roads

Throughout Mercer, Somerset, and Morris Counties are a series of boulders, tablets, and obelisks marking Washington's northward route after the battles at Trenton and Princeton.

Bernardsville

John Parker (or Vealtown) Tavern Site
Bernardsville Library
2 Morristown Road (Route 202)
(908) 766-0118

These days, the Bernardsville Library is best known for the ghost of Phyllis Parker, a young revolutionary-era woman, which supposedly appears among the bookshelves from time to time. Legend has it that Phyllis, the daughter of John Parker, lost her mind after seeing the mutilated body of her lover, who was hanged as a Tory spy.

But back in the old days, when Bernardsville was known as Vealtown, John Parker's Tavern was a favorite drinking spot of Continental army officers, including "Mad" Anthony Wayne. In fact, Old Army Road in Bernardsville seems to have come into being as a shortcut between Jockey Hollow and John Parker's back door. One reason the tavern was so friendly to the rebels was that Parker himself was a captain in the Somerset militia.

In front of the library is a stone tablet marking Washington's route to

John Parker Tavern Site, Bernardsville

MARK DI IONNO

Morristown following the battles at Trenton and Princeton in January 1777. There are a series of similar boulders, tablets, and obelisks throughout Mercer, Somerset, and Morris Counties.

Old Mill Inn
225 Route 202

On the site of this landmark restaurant was a large barn where grain for the troops at Jockey Hollow was stored.

Bound Brook

Battle of Bound Brook Monument
Hamilton and High Streets (the monument is in the cemetery here)

The Battle of Bound Brook actually took place at the Raritan River, about two blocks from the monument site, on April 13, 1777.

An outpost of about five hundred American soldiers under Maj. Gen. Benjamin Lincoln was in the area to defend Washington's main army at Morristown and the eight thousand British and Hessians in New Brunswick. Lord Cornwallis came out of New Brunswick with two thousand men and attacked at the river, planning to circle Lincoln's charges and gain control of the area. The Americans fought them off, but six of their troops were killed and anywhere from forty to eighty captured, including an artillery detachment and its guns. Cornwallis retreated before reinforcements arrived.

Frelinghuysen Tavern Site
213 East Main Street

On July 9, 1776, five days after the signing of the Declaration of Independence, Hendrick Fisher, the president of New Jersey's Provincial Congress, read the document to a gathering of local people.

A bronze plaque on the wall of what today is S. Klompus and Company describes the scene: "Upon completion of the reading the crowd went wild with joy, carrying Fisher on their shoulders through the village, while the Presbyterian Church bell rang loud and long, cannons fired, and rousing toasts were drunk by the lusty Patriots gathered there."

(For more on Fisher, see the Franklin section of this chapter.)

Middlebrook Encampment Site
Middlebrook Avenue

Perched on the south side of the first ridge of the Watchung Mountains, the Middlebrook encampment area was strategically important to Washington.

Middlebrook Encampment Site, Bound Brook

The encampment occupied much more than this site, with parts of the camp reaching down toward the Raritan River.

Washington brought the army here from Morristown on May 28, 1777, and stayed until July 2. He picked this spot to prevent the British from marching overland from New Brunswick to Philadelphia. On the high ground overlooking the Raritan River Valley toward New Brunswick, Washington found the perfect place. He could take his army east or south with ease or retreat back into the mountains if necessary.

The British general William Howe tried to lure Washington out of the stronghold by deploying troops from Middlesex County into lower Union County. Washington sent troops under the command of Lord Stirling to meet them, but kept the main army closer to Middlebrook. On June 26, 1777, in the Battle of Ash Swamp, also called the Battle of the Short Hills (see the Scotch Plains section of the Union County chapter), the Americans kept the British from closing off the pass back to Middlebrook, and Washington was able to get his army back to safety.

But the camp is best known for an event that is believed to have happened two weeks earlier. On June 14, 1777, Congress had approved the thirteen-star flag, designed by Betsy Ross, as the official flag of the United States of America. It is said that the Stars and Stripes first flew over the heads of the Continental army at Middlebrook. A replica of that flag flies over the Middlebrook campground day and night.

Washington's second stay, from December 11, 1778, to June 3, 1779, was uneventful. Even the weather cooperated, and the troops enjoyed a mild New Jersey winter as compared to the hard winters at Morristown and Valley Forge in other years.

Bridgewater

The Van Horne House
900 Main Street
PHONE: Unavailable.
HOURS: Unavailable.

During the second Middlebrook encampment, the home of Judge Philip Van Horne was the headquarters of Lord Stirling. It also hosted bigwigs from the other side—Cornwallis himself was a guest there at one time.

On the night of October 27, 1779, Col. John Simcoe, the British leader of a Tory group called the Queen's Rangers, began a rampage of Somerset

County by capturing a number of American officers at the Van Horne House. The rangers then burned a Dutch church near the Van Veghten House, proceeded south along what today is Route 533 to Millstone, and there burned the Somerset County Courthouse.

At this writing, the Van Horne House is owned by the county, and plans are being made to either hand it over to a social service group or allow a historic preservation group to run it.

The Van Veghten House
End of Van Veghten Road (off Finderne Avenue)
(908) 218-1281
HOURS: Tuesday, noon to 3 P.M., and the second Saturday of every
month from noon to 4 P.M.

This house, now operated by the Somerset County Historical Society, served as headquarters for Generals Nathaniel Greene and "Mad" Anthony Wayne during the second Middlebrook encampment. Wayne's Pennsylvania Line also camped on the house grounds. It was in this house that Washington danced with Mrs. Greene for three hours during a party in March 1779.

MARK DI IONNO

The Van Veghten House, Bridgewater

The house today is oddly situated at the end of an industrial road. But after you pass the tractor-trailer trucks and warehouses, the house suddenly appears on a dirt road in an idyllic setting: the pasture surrounding the house abuts the Raritan River, with cows, geese, and ducks all around.

The bridge over the Raritan River on Finderne Avenue (Route 533) is very close to the spot of the Van Veghten Bridge, where Simcoe's raiders fought with locals on the night of October 27, 1779.

Chimney Rock
Watchung Mountain County Park
Chimney Rock Road (Route 525)

It is said that Washington used this geologic oddity as a lookout point to keep tabs on British troop movements in the Raritan Valley.

Washington camped throughout the region of Chimney Rock Road and Washington Valley Road during the Middlebrook encampments. While he and the main army were in Morristown, these areas were used as outposts to keep the British in check.

Franklin

Battle Place (near Franklin High School)
Off Millstone Road near the intersection with Hamilton Street

Col. John Simcoe's rampage through Somerset County came to an end near this spot, when he and his rangers were ambushed by the New Jersey militia. Simcoe's reputation for quick-strike violence preceded him, and the minutemen were prepared for a bloody fight. Simcoe's horse was shot five times and crumpled beneath him. He was knocked unconscious in the fall. A Jersey militia captain and a ranger were killed. According to legend, one Jersey soldier wanted to stick his bayonet through Simcoe as he lay knocked out, but was persuaded not to. When Simcoe came to, he was a prisoner.

Despite the destruction and murder Simcoe left in his path (see the Hancock House entry in the Lower Alloways Creek Township section of the Lower Delaware chapter), he was exchanged for American officers two months later. After the war he became the first governor-general of Canada.

The Franklin Inn
538 Elizabeth Avenue
(732) 873-5244
HOURS: Wednesday, Saturday, and Sunday, 1 P.M. to 4 P.M.

This former stagecoach stop was the headquarters for General Cornwallis during a five-day British occupation of the area in June 1777. The British commander in chief, William Howe, may have also stopped there for a meeting with Cornwallis.

The restored inn today is a used-book store run by volunteers of the Meadows Foundation, a nonprofit Somerset County group that raises funds to purchase and restore historic properties in the area. All proceeds from the store go to the foundation.

Not far from the Franklin Inn is Colonial Park, where Cornwallis's troops camped during the occupation. The park can be reached from either Elizabeth Avenue or Amwell Road (Route 514).

Hendrick Fisher House
1960 Easton Avenue
(732) 356-0090
HOURS: By appointment.

Hendrick Fisher was no young radical. He was nearly eighty when the war started, but was still one of the most energetic and vocal opponents of the Crown. "Opponent" may be too mild a word. Hendrick Fisher (he is known as the "Samuel Adams of New Jersey") was an enemy of the Crown. And the feeling was mutual. When Gen. William Howe offered general amnesty to all Patriots early in the war, Hendrick Fisher and Abraham Staats (see the South Bound Brook section of this chapter) were two of only a handful of Jerseyans to whom amnesty did not apply. Instead, Fisher and Staats, who lived about a mile apart, were to be hanged on sight. The British tried to capture Fisher at this home in April 1777, but he was in hiding. Not finding him, they ransacked his house and barns and stole all his livestock. Fisher died in 1779 at age eighty-two and is buried in the family plot on the property. There is a historical marker in front of the house.

The Fisher House today is owned by the Ukrainian Orthodox Church and is part of the church's compound on Davidson Avenue. It serves as a private residence, but the church has restored it to reflect the colonial period and will arrange tours by appointment. The fact that Fisher was a freedom fighter is understandably important to the Ukrainians and they take great pride in owning and maintaining the home. The phone number listed above is the Consistory Business Office, which is open Monday through Friday.

Green Brook

Washington Rock State Park
Washington Avenue

High atop the first ridge of the Watchung Mountains is Washington Rock, where Washington spied on the British, especially during the first Middlebrook encampment. The park offers panoramic views of the Raritan Valley. Still, the question remains, how could Washington keep an eye on what the British were doing in New Brunswick, nine miles away? The answer is this: during the Revolution there were many fewer trees than there are today, because people used wood to build and for heat and cooking. In fact, accounts of local pillaging by armies of both sides often include the theft of firewood.

Also, when troops moved, the wagons and artillery kicked up a significant amount of dust.

The 1912 Daughters of the American Revolution plaque in the fieldstone monument-flagpole at the lookout site carries the wonderful, eternal motto of Revolutionary War preservationists everywhere: "Lest We Forget."

The View from Washington Rock, Green Brook

Griggstown

Honeyman House
1008 Canal Road
(Private)

Hidden behind a patch of tall shrubs and trees is a modest white clapboard home with blue shutters. As a Revolutionary War site, the house is one of New Jersey's best-kept secrets—fittingly, considering that its colonial-era owner was one of Washington's best-kept secret weapons.

Honeyman had been a British soldier in the French and Indian Wars, serving heroically under Gen. James Wolfe. Washington is said to have been familiar with Honeyman's war record and either enlisted or permitted him to work for him as a spy. Honeyman went to work for the British in Trenton as a butcher and became friendly with Col. Johann Rall, commander of the Hessians there. After a few weeks studying troop movements and readiness, Honeyman wandered into the woods on a cold December night in 1776. He was captured by American scouts after a struggle that left his face bruised and his tied wrists bleeding, and was transported into Pennsylvania to Washington's camp.

MARK DI IONNO

The House of John Honeyman, Griggstown

In front of the sentries, Washington berated Honeyman and threatened him with hanging. He then dismissed the guards for about a half hour, during which time Honeyman gave him the lay of land in Trenton. When the guards returned, Honeyman was dragged off to the guardhouse—which was conveniently left unlocked. Honeyman then "found" a horse, and later a boat to take him back across the Delaware.

He reported to Rall and showed him his bruises. Rall questioned him about the condition of the American army and Honeyman told him they were shoeless, demoralized, and ready to mutiny.

A few days later, Washington led his army into Trenton on Christmas Day, surprised the Hessians, and turned the tide of the war.

Honeyman was arrested twice more during the war and charged with high treason, but each time won release. He eventually moved to Lamington, where he farmed and raised livestock and died at age ninety-five. He is buried in the Lamington Presbyterian Church Cemetery.

Liberty Corner

Liberty Pole Site
Liberty Corner Road

In the village center is a triangular green where a boulder with a bronze plaque commemorates a Liberty Pole raised here by local Patriots. The French army commanded by Count Rochambeau camped near here on its march to Yorktown in 1781.

Millstone

Burned Courthouse Site
13 South River Road

After burning the Dutch church near Van Veghten's Bridge in the Finderne section of what today is Bridgewater, Simcoe's raiders turned south toward Millstone, which was the county seat at the time.

Simcoe and his men rode down the west bank of the Millstone on a route that parallels Route 533 today. At Millstone, they broke into the courthouse, freed three Loyalist prisoners there, and set fire to the building. As the courthouse went up in flames, winds carried embers into surrounding buildings.

The site of the courthouse is now a private home at 13 South River Road, near the intersection of Main Street (Route 533) and Amwell Road (514) in

Millstone Courthouse Raid Site

the village of Millstone. South River Road intersects with Amwell Road about 100 yards east of Main Street. At the site is a large boulder with a state of New Jersey bronze plaque mounted on it. The plaque gives the date of the attack as October 26, but most accounts say it happened a day later.

Pluckemin

The Jacobus Vanderveer House
Route 202/206 (just south of River Road)

This house was the headquarters of Gen. Henry Knox, Washington's three-hundred-pound chief of artillery, who hid the fact that he had blown off two fingers in a hunting accident by constantly wrapping the mutilated hand in a handkerchief.

Knox was the Continental army's big-gun expert. During the siege of Boston, Knox and his men transported more than sixty tons of weaponry—shells and about fifty heavy guns—down from Fort Ticonderoga in the dead of winter. The heavy artillery helped persuade the British to give up the siege.

His job in Pluckemin was less daunting but equally important. He brought sixteen hundred men to the Watchungs to train them in the use of artillery and military tactics. (See the Artillery Park entry in this section.)

Knox had great administrative qualities and was loyal to Washington. After the war, he became the country's first secretary of war. Like Lord Stirling, he survived the dangers of the battlefield only to die a strange death at a young age—when he was fifty-six a chicken bone perforated his intestines.

At this writing the Vanderveer house is in disrepair, but it has been stabilized by Bedminster Township, which includes the Village of Pluckemin. The township is planning to open the house as a museum to house artifacts from Artillery Park sometime in the future. An organization called the Friends of the Vanderveer/Knox House has been established to raise funds for the restoration of the house and the creation of the museum. For more information, call the township at (908) 234-0333, ext. 14.

Artillery Park
The Hills (housing complex)
Route 202/206 and vicinity

The Hills development is often cited as an example of suburban sprawl gone haywire: thousands of condominium units piled high up on a fifteen-hundred-acre mountain side, destroying the landscape and having nothing short of electric-shock impact on the surrounding community. Add another strike against this development: it covers one of the most important Revolutionary War archaeological sites in the country.

Artillery Camp was on the south side of the mountain about midway up. It has been called the nation's first military academy, and to some extent that's true.

Knox brought sixteen hundred men here to train them in military strategy and tactics and in the use of heavy artillery. The center of the camp was an E-shaped building. About fourteen smaller buildings housed the main repair shops for American guns of all sizes.

On February 18, 1779, Knox threw one of the most famous parties of the period, a celebration of the first anniversary of the French intervention in the war. Knox hosted about four hundred American officers, including Washington, in a hundred-foot-long pavilion that was built for the occasion. He treated them to a fireworks display and an extravagant ball. (A description of Washington's attire contradicts his reputation for stoical dignity: he wore a black velvet suit with a steel rapier and knee and shoe buckles, and his hair was powdered, pulled straight back, tied in a black silk bag, and decorated with a rosette.)

With the support of the development company, Rutgers anthropology professor John L. Seidel began an archaeological dig at the site in 1981. Ten thousand artifacts were found, including muskets, bayonets, horseshoes, buttons, dinnerware, pistol shot, gun parts, pieces of sword blades, and the remains of gunsmith, tinsmith, and carpenter shops. Two engraved brass tips from officers' sword belts bear early depictions of the Stars and Stripes.

The site now is a wooded area surrounded by the residential condo complex.

Washington's Route Markers

There are two markers in Pluckemin on the route Washington took to Morristown following the Battle of Princeton. The first is at the intersection of Route 202/206 and Washington Valley Road. The marker is on a low-lying boulder in front of the A&P parking lot.

The second marker, just north of the first on Route 202/206, stands near the site of the Fenner House. There Washington wrote to Congress

MARK DI IONNO

Washington Route Marker, Pluckemin

describing his victories at Princeton and Trenton. He also explained that he had thought of attacking the British at New Brunswick but "the danger of losing the advantage we had gained, by aiming at too much, induced me . . . to abandon the attempt."

The army camped throughout Pluckemin on the night of January 5, 1777, but the main body stayed along Chambers Brook on the Bridgewater-Bedminster border (just north of The Manor restaurant on Route 202/206).

Also in the village, at the site of the current Pluckemin Presbyterian Church, was St. Paul's Lutheran Church, which had been vandalized by the British early in the war. On the army's march to Morristown, the two hundred thirty British captured at Princeton were herded into the church, which served as a one-night prison.

Rocky Hill

Rockingham
Route 518 at Kingston–Rocky Hill Road
(609) 921-8835
HOURS: Wednesday through Saturday, 10 A.M. to noon and
1 P.M. to 4 P.M.; Sundays, 1 P.M. to 4 P.M.

MARK DI IONNO

*A Young Colonial
at Rockingham,
Rocky Hill*

The Docents of Rockingham, Rocky Hill

If you want to get a small child interested in history, Rockingham is the place to go. Peggy Carlsen, the on-site historian and curator at this state-owned site, runs a continuous schedule of kid-oriented programs and demonstrations. She also has a junior docent program in which young teenagers staff an outbuilding on the property where kids can dress up in colonial clothing, play eighteenth-century children's games, and even do a few old-time chores. Next door is a colonial kitchen, where volunteer docents cook full colonial meals using ingredients from Rockingham's authentic eighteenth-century garden.

The house has impressive historical significance, too. One of New Jersey's "Washington's Headquarters," it was the place where the general officially retired as commander of the Continental army.

Washington came to Rocky Hill on August 23, 1783, at the request of Congress, which was convening at Nassau Hall in Princeton and wanted his input on military matters. There was no place available in Princeton that could accommodate Washington and his staff, so he moved into this two-story frame house (which has been restored to its drab olive color).

On his five-mile trips to Princeton, the streets were often lined with people hailing this new national hero.

It is thought that on November 2, from the second-floor porch of the house, Washington read his farewell orders to his 150-man Life Guard and staff. Copies of those orders hang in the entrance hall at Rockingham.

Like so many other New Jersey historic sites, Rockingham narrowly escaped razing. The house was originally closer to the Millstone River, on property owned by a rock quarrying firm. One hundred years after Washington stayed there, the house was reduced to a shack, serving as a bunkhouse for quarry workers. As the mountain the house stood on began to be eaten away, plans were made to knock it down. The Washington Headquarters Association was formed, and the house was moved a quarter of a mile up the hill, restored, and opened to the public in 1897. It was moved again in 1956, and a third relocation is planned for 2001. The house will be closed for about a year, and then will reopen at its new site on Route 603 (Laurel Road) on property owned by the Delaware and Raritan Canal State Park, with a walking trail connecting to the towpath near Kingston.

Somerville

The Wallace House
65 Washington Place
(908) 725-1015
HOURS: Wednesday through Saturday, 10 A.M. to noon and
1 P.M. to 4 P.M.; Sundays, 1 P.M. to 4 P.M.

Now a state historic site, the Wallace House was used by Washington during the Middlebrook encampment in the winter and spring of 1778–79. With the war in the colonies at something of a standstill, Washington decided to dispatch troops to northern Pennsylvania and western New York State, where the Iroquois Indians' Six Nations Confederation and Loyalist forces were attacking American frontier towns and outposts.

In response to two incidents—the massacres at Cherry Valley, New York, and Wyoming Valley, Pennsylvania—Washington sent Maj. Gen. John Sullivan from Easton, Pennsylvania, northwest to Fort Niagara, the British stronghold in New York state. The language in Washington's orders was uncharacteristically harsh: he wanted "total destruction and devastation"; he wanted Iroquois country not "merely overrun, but destroyed" and "the capture of as many prisoners of every age and sex as possible."

In Sullivan's Expedition about four thousand Continental army troops punched through the frontier, burning and destroying about forty Iroquois settlements, including their orchards and fields. The Iroquois retreated to Fort Niagara, which Sullivan never reached. Still, the operation was a success. While Iroquois harassment continued, the Six Nations Confederation was never able to muster its earlier power. American colonists were able to push westward and populate the region.

The house was built by John Wallace, a wealthy fabric importer and merchant from Philadelphia. Wallace's eight-room mansion—on 107 acres that fronted the Old York Road—was the biggest house in the Bound Brook area. Like the Ford Mansion in Morristown, the Wallace House was nearly brand new when Washington and his staff came to stay. Visitors to the house included the Marquis de Lafayette, Baron von Steuben, Alexander Hamilton, and Benedict Arnold.

Washington was here for six months, except for a six-week trip to Philadelphia, where he addressed Congress. Mrs. Washington was there with him for much of the time, and they socialized in the area with a number of prominent citizens, including Jacob Hardenberg, the pastor of the Dutch Reformed Church.

The Old Dutch Parsonage
38 Washington Place
(908) 725-1015
HOURS: Wednesday through Saturday, 10 A.M. to noon and
       1 P.M. to 4 P.M.; Sundays, 1 P.M. to 4 P.M.

Adjacent to the Wallace House is the Old Dutch Parsonage, home to Jacob Hardenberg. Washington was an occasional guest here. Hardenberg, a supporter of independence, worked as a peacemaker between the army and local residents who felt inconvenienced by its presence. He was also instrumental in the formation of Queen's College (Rutgers University) in 1766. He became the first president of the college in 1785.

He was the stepfather of Capt. Frederick Frelinghuysen, the Somerset County militiaman who is credited for the shot that killed the Hessian commander, Johann Rall, during the Battle of Trenton. The parsonage was Frelinghuysen's boyhood home.

In 1913, after it was scheduled for demolition by the Central Railroad of New Jersey, the house was moved a few hundred feet to its present site—another historic landmark that narrowly escaped razing.

(Note: Visitors to the Old Dutch Parsonage must first check in at the Wallace House.)

Washington's Route Marker
Corner of Main and Warren Streets

Throughout Mercer, Somerset, and Morris Counties are a series of boulders, tablets, and obelisks marking Washington's route following the battles at Trenton and Princeton. One of these is at this corner, across from the Somerset County Courthouse and the Somerset Hotel.

The Somerset Hotel stands on the spot of Tunison's Tavern, where Washington housed some of his officers while he was at the Wallace House.

South Bound Brook

The Staats House
17 Von Steuben Lane
(732) 356-0258 (South Bound Brook Borough Hall)
HOURS: Unavailable.

Like his neighbor Hendrick Fisher, Abraham Staats was so much hated by the British that their troops were ordered to hang him on sight. Unlike Fisher, who was a visible and vocal enemy of the crown, Staats played a somewhat mysterious role in the Revolution.

An enduring legend says that Staats, an unassuming surveyor and tax collector, was the head of a spy ring so pervasive and damaging that the British labeled him an "archtraitor."

The legend says Staats had a slave named Tory Jack, who would go to the taverns of New Brunswick and eavesdrop on the conversations of British officers. He would then return to Staats and tell him what he heard, and Staats, in turn, would tell his contacts in the Continental army.

Staats allowed his home to be used by Baron Frederick William von Steuben, the Prussian officer who came to teach Washington's army the nuances of modern warfare. Von Steuben taught Washington's officers the technical aspects of open field warfare, and the officers in turn instilled in the men the discipline and technique that enabled them to fight the highly trained British army to a standstill in the meadows of Monmouth. While at the Staats House, von Steuben wrote the *Regulations for the Infantry of the United States.*

At this writing the Staats House is in the process of being purchased by the town. It will eventually be turned into a period museum, with information on its two famous inhabitants.

There will also be some archaeological digs on the four-acre site to see if Staats, the spy, left any clues behind.

Union County

Union County was an important place during the Revolution, politically and strategically. There was more war-related action there than in any other county in the state except for Mercer.

The Elizabethtown (now Elizabeth) area was the leading social and intellectual city in New Jersey. The upper echelon of its citizens included people like Elias Boudinot, the Reverend James Caldwell, Abraham Clark, the Crane family, the Daytons (father Elias and son Jonathan), William Livingston, and the Ogden clan—all strongly opposed to English intervention in the affairs of the colonies. Also firmly entrenched in the area were very prominent Loyalists. Right down the street from the First Presbyterian Church where Caldwell preached independence, the Reverend Thomas Bradbury Chandler told his congregation at St. John's Episcopal Church that they should stay true to the crown. Much of the rest of the county was the same way.

When the British tried to drive a wedge through the state, Union County was the place they attacked. At different times during the war, Union County was what basically stood between the British in New York and New Brunswick and Washington in the Watchungs. Each time the British made moves to get to Washington in his mountain hideouts, they had to cross Union County to do it, resulting in battles at Connecticut Farms (Union), Springfield, and Ash Swamp (in Scotch Plains).

Clark

Homestead Farm
Oak Ridge Golf Club
Oak Ridge Road
(732) 574-0139

The Oak Ridge Golf Club lies to the south of the Ash Brook Golf Course. Both are operated by Union County.

The land on the two courses encompasses the Ash Swamp, where a significant battle was fought on June 26, 1777. A monument to the battle—known as the Battle of the Short Hills—is at the entrance to Ash Brook (see the Battle of the Short Hills Monument entry in the Scotch Plains section of this chapter). But the first fighting began on the land that today is the Oak Ridge Golf Club.

In the early morning of June 26, the New Jersey militia began to harass the British troops encamped near what is today the intersection of Inman Avenue and Featherbed Lane in Edison. (Oak Ridge Road in Clark becomes Featherbed Lane.)

The British cavalry gave chase. The Americans lured them into the Ash Swamp, where their horses got mired in the muck. And the battle began.

Clark historian Bill Fidurski says you can make a case that the Battle of the Short Hills was the first clash where Americans defended the Stars and Stripes.

"The flag resolution was adopted by the Continental Congress at Philadelphia twelve days earlier," he says, "and there were no significant engagements anywhere in the colonies between that time and the battle at the swamp.

"We don't know if the American troops at Ash Swamp fought under the Stars and Stripes, but you can say figuratively at least that they were the first to defend it."

A defense of a more personal kind had happened at the Homestead Farm house eighteen months earlier. The British came through the area as they moved from Hackensack to New Brunswick in the fall of 1776. Farm owner William Smith heard his daughter, Isabel, screaming for help from the home. He burst in to find her being molested by a Hessian officer, whom he killed. The Hessian's fellow officers shot Smith twice, but he survived and was never prosecuted.

Elizabeth

Minuteman Monument
Elizabeth Avenue at Bank Square

In the middle of one of Elizabeth's busiest intersections is a monument to the heavy action that took place in Union County between June 7 and June 23, 1780.

On the night of June 6, Lt. Gen. Baron Wilhelm von Knyphausen, a Prussian, led the British army in his command from Staten Island to a landing at DeHart's point in Elizabethtown. Knyphausen had plans to roll through the plains and mountain passes of the Watchungs to Morristown, where he would attack Washington's main army.

Knyphausen had good reason to believe he would succeed. The main American army was down to four thousand men, and in May two regiments of the Connecticut Line had mutinied. The area east of Morristown was

MARK DI IONNO

Elizabethtown Monument

filled with Tories and Loyalists who were ready to help the British crush their Patriot neighbors. Those same Patriots, Knyphausen believed, were tired of the war and just needed an excuse to lay down their arms.

The Minuteman Monument plaque, dedicated in 1905, tells the first part of the story of one of the most critical months of the Revolution:

> On this spot at daybreak June 7, 1780, began the fighting against the British Forces moving toward Springfield. Here fell Gen. Stirling at the head of the advancing column on June 8, after the British retreat from Springfield. Gen. Hand here attacked and drove back the 22nd Regt. to the British main position at the point. Skirmishing on this ground continued until the British retreat to Staten Island, June 23rd.

The rest of the story will unfold through descriptions of sites in Elizabeth, Union (then known as Connecticut Farms), and Springfield.

The First Presbyterian Church
Broad Street and Caldwell Place
(908) 353-1518

Months before the Knyphausen invasion, an Elizabethtown native and English Loyalist named Cornelius Hatfield Jr. led a raiding party from Staten Island—a haven for British-sympathizers—to his hometown.

Hatfield, a British spy and scout for most of the war, led the marauders to the First Presbyterian Church, one of the most inspirational institutions of the Revolution.

The congregation of this church was led by the Reverend James Caldwell, known as the Fighting Parson. Caldwell was an energetic and combative Patriot—an enemy of the local Tories and Loyalists to the point that they put a price on his head.

Caldwell's congregation was also fiercely patriotic. Thirty-six men in the congregation were commissioned officers in the Continental army and many more served. A list of the congregants reads like a *Who's Who* of the American Revolution in New Jersey. They included Elias Boudinot, president of the Continental Congress (1782–83); Abraham Clark, a signer of the Declaration of Independence; Gen. William Crane; Col. Elias Dayton, a hero of the Battle of Springfield; Dayton's son, Capt. Jonathan Dayton, the youngest signer of the U.S. Constitution; Gen. Philemon Dickinson; William Livingston, the first governor of New Jersey and a signer of the Constitution (see the Liberty Hall entry in the Union section of this chapter); and Gen. Matthias Ogden.

Another staunch patriot in the congregation was Cornelius Hatfield Sr., the father of Cornelius Jr. The Hatfields provide evidence that loyalties sometimes split families during the American Revolution.

On the night of January 25, 1780, Cornelius Hatfield Jr. led a raiding party into Elizabethtown. They captured a garrison of fifty Americans, burned the courthouse and the Presbyterian Church, and escaped to Staten Island. Witnesses say Cornelius Hatfield Jr. himself started the fire at the church.

The senior Hatfield allowed the congregation to assemble in his barn until 1786, when a new church was built. At the end of the Revolution, the junior Hatfield moved to England. Returning in 1807 to claim his father's estate, he soon found himself on trial for the murder of a man he had ordered hanged during the war. He was acquitted under the terms of the peace treaty and moved back to England.

On the grounds of the current church is the site of the Old Academy, which was attended by Aaron Burr and Alexander Hamilton. A small iron plaque topped by a man on horseback marks the spot.

Presbyterian Church Cemetery
(next to the church)

There is a monument here to the Reverend James Caldwell and his wife, Hannah. She is said to have been killed by a British soldier at Connecticut Farms during a skirmish on June 7, 1780 (see the Union section of this chapter), although the monument says June 8. The monument was erected in 1845 by the Society of the Cincinnati.

Also buried here is Shepard Kollock, a Continental army officer who fought at Trenton and Monmouth and who published the first newspaper in northern New Jersey. The paper, called the *New-Jersey Journal,* was decidedly pro-Patriot. It was published in Chatham, a Revolutionary stronghold, in 1779 (see the Morris County chapter). In 1786 Kollock moved his operation to Elizabethtown to the vicinity of what is today 39 Broad Street. His paper became the *Daily Journal,* which was the oldest active newspaper in the country until it folded in 1992. Kollock died in 1846 at age eighty-eight.

Union County Courthouse
2 Broad Street

Next door to the Presbyterian Church cemetery is the Union County Courthouse. It stands on the site of the old borough courthouse, which was burned down by the British on the same night as the church.

The Caldwells' Burial Site Monument

It is said that the new courthouse is haunted by the ghost of Hannah Caldwell. Over the years, a number of late night workers and maintenance crew members say they have seen an apparition of a woman in a white flowing gown floating down the hall.

On the courthouse lawn is a cannon taken from the British at Stony Point, New York, by units of the Continental army including the militia from Elizabethtown. A plaque, placed by the Sons of the American Revolution in 1905, tells the story:

> This gun, cast in Strasbourg in 1758, was sent by Louis XV, King of France, to Canada for the defense of Quebec. Upon the surrender of that place in the following years, the gun fell into the hands of the British. In April, 1760, the French recaptured the gun. And in May the British retook it. In the fall of 1775 this gun aided in the repulse of the Continental force under Gen. Richard Montgomery, who was mortally wounded while attempting to capture it. In June, 1779, Sir Henry Clinton captured Stony Point, and a month later Gen. Anthony Wayne retook it finding this gun among the trophies. Gen. Washington presented the piece to troops from Elizabethtown who had acted as a reserve, and it was brought here by them soon after.

Elizabeth Public Library
11 South Broad Street (across from the courthouse)

The library is built on the site of the Red Lion Inn, where a reception was held for Washington on April 23, 1789, as he made his way to New York for his inauguration as president.

Boxwood Hall (Boudinot Mansion)
1073 East Jersey Street
(973) 648-4540 (Note: Boxwood Hall has a 973 area code because it
    has a Newark phone exchange).
HOURS: Monday through Friday, 9 A.M. to noon, and 1 P.M. to 5 P.M.
    Because of staffing shortages, it is always best to call first to
    find out if the house is open.

Few houses in New Jersey have histories as rich as Boxwood Hall.

Elias Boudinot, president of the Continental Congress, lived here from 1772 to 1795. The young Alexander Hamilton stayed with Boudinot while attending the Old Academy.

After the Reverend James Caldwell was murdered, his body was brought to Boudinot's home. Boudinot eulogized the Fighting Parson in an impassioned speech to American troops stationed in Elizabethtown.

MARK DI IONNO

Boxwood Hall

Boudinot, a signer of the peace treaty with England, hosted George Washington at Boxwood in the days before Washington's inauguration. And while Washington may be the father of the country, Boudinot is the father of one of its warmest traditions. It was Boudinot who drafted a resolution calling for a national day of thanks. Washington agreed and Thanksgiving Day was born.

Boudinot was a protégé of Princeton's Richard Stockton, a signer of the Declaration of Independence, and the men married each other's sister.

Jonathan Dayton bought the house from Boudinot in 1795. While he was Speaker of the House of Representatives and, later, a member of the Senate, he hosted people like the Marquis de Lafayette.

Boxwood, which is a state historic site, has artifacts from Dayton's days, including a military uniform owned by him.

Dayton is buried on the grounds of St. John's Episcopal Church at 61 Broad Street. A brick monument with a bronze plaque, celebrating the 150th anniversary of the signing of the U.S. Constitution, was placed there by the Daughters of the American Revolution in 1937.

Belcher-Ogden Mansion
1046 East Jersey Street
(908) 351-2500
HOURS: By appointment.

Up the street from Boxwood is the Belcher-Ogden Mansion, which is operated and maintained by the Elizabethtown Historical Foundation.

The house was built on land owned by John Ogden, one of Elizabethtown's founding fathers. The royal governor of New Jersey, Jonathan Belcher, lived here for ten years before his death in 1757. During that time he laid the groundwork for the College of New Jersey, which in time became Princeton University.

In 1778, Washington, Hamilton, and Lafayette visited the house for the wedding of Boudinot's brother, Elisha.

The house was later inhabited by Aaron Ogden, who was New Jersey's governor in 1812–13.

Site of Dr. William Barnet House
(later the General Winfield Scott House)
Corner of East Jersey Street and Madison Avenue

Winfield Scott was a leading military figure in the Mexican War and also the Civil War, but since this is a book about the Revolutionary War, we'll concentrate on Dr. William Barnet.

Barnet was a friend of Washington's and a surgeon in the Continental army. He lived at this site between 1763 and 1790. The British ransacked his house in 1781, and according to *The WPA Guide* (see the Research chapter) the doctor assessed the damage like this: "They emptied my feather beds in the street, broke in windows, smashed my mirrors, and left our pantry and storeroom department bare. I could forgive them all that, but the rascals stole from my kitchen wall the finest string of red peppers in all Elizabeth."

New Providence

Presbyterian Church Cemetery
Springfield and Passaic Avenues (across from South Street)

Behind the Presbyterian Church is an extensive cemetery that contains the remains of forty-eight Continental army soldiers. A Sons of the American Revolution memorial plaque, placed in a pudding-stone boulder in 1928, is next to the driveway on the Passaic Avenue side right behind the church.

Plainfield

Drake House Museum

602 West Front Street
(908) 755-5831
HOURS: Sundays, 2 P.M. to 4 P.M., and by appointment.

Back in the 1930s, the Drake House was billed as a "Washington Headquarters," but accurate history has since prevailed.

"We do believe George Washington visited here and that he was friendly with the home's owner, Nathaniel Drake," said Lisa Crawley, the education coordinator at the house. "We know from the oral family history of Nathaniel Drake's daughter, Phoebe, that Washington visited the house around 1777, when Phoebe was 17."

The WPA Guide (see the Research chapter) says Washington was a frequent visitor during "reconnoitering expeditions into the plains E[ast] of town," although there is no known documentation.

Crawley says there is strong circumstantial evidence that Washington stayed here. Washington and Drake had a good mutual friend in a local minister, and on maps drawn by Robert Erskine (see the Passaic County chapter) the Drake House—like certain homes that are known to have been frequented by the general—was marked with a star.

The Drake House, built in 1746 and now operated by the Plainfield and North Plainfield Historical Society, has a Revolutionary War–era kitchen and bedroom. The bedroom is called the "Washington bedroom."

However, the most notable piece in the Drake House is the seven-by-nine-foot Julian Scott painting in the library. Scott was a famous Civil War–era artist who lived and worked in Plainfield. This giant work, *The Death of Gen. Sedgwick*, was purchased by New York banker John S. Harberger, who bought the Drake House in 1864.

Blue Hills Fort Marker

Green Brook Park
Plainfield

Not far from the Drake House, in the eastern tip of Green Brook Park, is a Daughters of the American Revolution marker locating the site of the Blue Hills fort.

The Blue Hills fort was a large outpost that protected the paths leading to greater American troop concentrations ensconced in the Watchungs. The fort was continually under assault until the British withdrew from the area.

To find the marker, enter the park on West End Avenue. On Park Road, right before the playground, is a huge green bush that comes up almost to the street. The marker is partially covered by that bush.

 Rahway

Merchants and Drovers Tavern
1632 St. Georges Avenue
(908) 381-0441
HOURS: By appointment.

The former tavern and stagecoach stop, now operated by the Rahway Historical Society, was visited by Washington on his way to New York City to be inaugurated as president in April 1789. A plaque outside tells the story.

First Presbyterian Church Cemetery
1731 Church Street (off St. Georges Avenue)

Here lies Declaration of Independence signer Abraham Clark, his grave marked and restored by the Daughters of the American Revolution in 1924. Clark is buried alongside his wife, Sarah, who died in 1804, ten years after her husband. A granite boulder holds both of their grave markers.

 Roselle

Abraham Clark House
101 West Ninth Avenue
(908) 486-1783
HOURS: By appointment.

Born in Elizabethtown, Abraham Clark lived his entire life on a farm where this neighborhood is now. The Abraham Clark House is a replica of the original Clark House, which was on land on the next block east, between 116 and 120 Crane Street.

Clark was an outspoken critic of the Crown and a staunch defender of the principle of inalienable rights. He was a delegate to the Second Continental Congress, where he voted to ratify the Declaration of Independence and then signed it.

Inside the Clark House is a small museum with replica items from the period and a few documents signed by Clark, who was a lawyer.

"They're just legal documents he signed pertaining to local deed transfers, nothing pertaining to the Revolution or the Declaration of Independence," said Robert Reynolds, the state registrar for the Sons of the American Revolution, who use the house as their headquarters.

The Sons also maintain a genealogical library here.

Roselle Park

Galloping Hill Road Monument
Galloping Hill Road and Colonial Road

One block north of Westfield Avenue (Route 28) on the Roselle Park–Elizabeth border is a small granite monument on the front yard of a private home at 130 Galloping Hill Road.

It is a Daughters of the American Revolution monument, placed in 1913. The inscription says, "Here the British turned into Galloping Hill Road from Elizabethtown to Connecticut Farms and Springfield at the time of the battles June 7 and 23, 1780. The son of Gen. William Crane is said to have been bayoneted to death by British soldiers near this spot."

Washington afterwards said of the New Jersey militia, "They flew to arms universally and acted with a spirit equal to anything I have seen during the war."

MARK DI IONNO

"The British Turned Here" Marker, Roselle Park

Scotch Plains

Battle of the Short Hills Monument
(This battle is also known as the Battle of Ash Swamp)
Raritan Road

At the entrance to Union County's Ash Brook Golf Course is a stone monument with a cannon perched on top. Four panels covered in plastic tell the story of the Battle of the Short Hills, including the names of some local men who fought there.

The battle, which took place on June 26, 1777, was a significant encounter with large numbers of troops involved, but it is the least known of New Jersey's large-scale Revolutionary War conflicts.

The monument explains:

On the 26th of June in 1777 Washington's Continental forces of under 6,000 men fought a running battle on the plains below the Watchung Mountains with the combined British and Hessian troops numbering 12,000.

Early on that Thursday morning the British, under the command of Gen. William Howe, after feigning a departure from New Jersey, suddenly at midnight began to march upon the rebel army that had left their mountain camp to come to the low country at Swamp Town [South Plainfield], Quibble Town [Piscataway–North Plainfield] and the outposts in The Short Hills and Ash Swamp [Scotch Plains] in order to meet the British. . . .

Lord Stirling divided by Cornwallis drew his troops into battle formation on rising ground near Ash Swamp determined to make a stand.

His force of 1,798 men included Gen. 'William Scotch' Maxwell's Brigade consisting of four New Jersey regiments. . . .

Outnumbered by Howe's full forces with at least 15 cannons, the Americans stood their ground but the superiority of arms and numbers forced them to withdraw.

The most important fact is left out: Lord Stirling's stand allowed Washington's main army to escape safely to Middlebrook. (See the Somerset County chapter.)

Frazee Homestead
Corner of Raritan and Terrill Roads
(Private)

It is said that Gen. Charles Cornwallis stopped by this house during the Battle of the Short Hills, lured by the smell of baking bread. When he asked the owner, Betty Frazee, if he and his guards could have some, she replied,

"Your lordship will please understand that I give this bread in fear, not in love."

Cornwallis—ever the officer and gentleman—declined to take the bread and moved on.

The Osborn Cannonball House
1840 Front Street
(908) 232-1199
HOURS: First Sunday of every month, 2 P.M. to 4 P.M.,
        except January and February. Tours by appointment.

Occupants of the Osborn House during the Revolution had a close-up view of the action as both American and British troops passed by on the busy main road outside. In at least one incident the view was too good, as an American cannonball fired during a skirmish hit the house. The house is operated by the Historical Society of Scotch Plains and Fanwood.

The Spence House
1461 Martine Avenue
(Private)

The Spence house has no outside markings, but it is easy to find: it is a Georgian mansion in a neighborhood of smaller post–World War II homes.

According to *The WPA Guide* (see the Research chapter) the house, "built in 1774, was used during the Revolution by American soldiers. A strong room in the cellar with the name 'George Washington' carved on a beam is believed to have served as a prison cell."

The current owners, the Plumeri family, have had the house for eighteen years. When interviewed they said they knew the house had some historical significance, but they had never seen or heard of the "George Washington" carving.

There may be something to the legend, though. The house is less than a mile from the Battle of the Short Hills site, and in times when houses were few and far between, the armies would have taken any shelter or conveniences available to them.

Springfield

The Presbyterian Church
Morris Avenue and Church Mall

The church is near the place where the Continental army made its final stand during the Battle of Springfield on June 23, 1780 (see the Union section of this chapter).

MARK DI IONNO

*First Presbyterian
Church, Springfield*

    The current church was built in 1791 to replace the one burned by the British as they retreated through Springfield and back to Staten Island, effectively ending all major fighting in New Jersey.

    It was at the church that the Reverend James Caldwell, the Fighting Parson, ripped the pages from the hymnals of the famous hymn-writer Isaac Watts and handed them out to the troops so they could wad their muskets. As the British approached, Caldwell supposedly said, "Now give 'em Watts, boys!"

    Caldwell wasn't the only hero of the day. Col. Israel Angell's outnumbered Rhode Island regiment slowed the British at the Rahway River Bridge on what today is Morris Avenue, and Col. "Light-Horse" Harry Lee did the same at Vauxhall Road. (See the Union section of this chapter.)

The fierce fighting took a lot out of the British. It was in the neighborhood of the church that Baron von Knyphausen, having met much stronger resistance than he anticipated for the second time in sixteen days, decided to withdraw.

The Presbyterian Church Cemetery
Morris Avenue and Church Mall

Across the street from the west side of the church and behind a public parking lot is the church cemetery, which contains graves of soldiers killed in the Battle of Springfield. It is marked by a Sons of the American Revolution plaque on the brick entranceway. The plaque was dedicated on June 23, 1930, on the 150th anniversary of the battle.

Cemetery
39 Mountain Avenue

Across Morris Avenue from the Presbyterian Church is a strip mall called the "Gen. Green [*sic*] Shopping Center." Just south of that shopping center (which is on part of the battleground), on Mountain Avenue, is a small cemetery. The cemetery, above street level, is sandwiched between an architects'

Daughters of the American Revolution Cemetery, Springfield

building at 37 Mountain Avenue and a business-use home at 41 Mountain Avenue.

The cemetery is the final resting place of soldiers killed in the Battle of Springfield and others who served but died later. A Daughters of the American Revolution plaque and a marble Sons of the American Revolution monument are located here.

The Cannonball House (The Hutching House)
126 Morris Avenue
(973) 376-4784
HOURS: By appointment.

Standing between two modern commercial buildings on an extremely busy road, the Cannonball House is truly one of the grand old survivors from colonial times.

First, it was hit by a cannonball during the fighting at Springfield. Second, it was one of only four homes not burned by the British as they retreated from town. (The British are believed to have used it as a temporary hospital.) Now, more than two centuries later, it has withstood years of neglect and nearby overdevelopment, including smog and truck vibrations from Morris Avenue. The paint is peeling, the masonry is cracking, and there is garbage piled up in the back. Operated by the Springfield Historical Society, the house has no regular hours. However, the main attraction can be seen without entering: on the west wall hanging from a bracket is the baseball-sized cannonball that lodged in the house during the fighting.

Summit

The "Old Sow" Plaque
226 Hobart Avenue
(between Beacon Road and the Beacon Hill Country Club)

Route 24 climbs out of Springfield up the first ridge of the Watchung Mountains through what is known as Hobart Gap. To the north is Short Hills, to the south Summit.

On Hobart Road in Summit, less than five hundred yards from the highway, is a mound of high ground known as Beacon Hill.

Here Lord Stirling, under orders from Washington, positioned a signal beacon—part of a system of twenty-three bonfire beacons built in the Watchungs and other high points through New Jersey that warned American militia about the advance of British troops.

Near the beacon was a cannon nicknamed "Old Sow." Before the Battle of Springfield, "Old Sow" was fired a number of times, calling the local militia to arms. In 1896, the Sons of the American Revolution put a plaque on a boulder at the site. When a home was built here in 1907, the plaque and boulder were incorporated into a stone wall in the front yard, surrounded by ivy.

"Old Sow" is in the weapon room of the main museum at Washington's Headquarters at the Morristown National Historical Park, where a placard explains that it is actually a "Crown Prince" cast-iron six-pound cannon of English origin. Some of the cannonballs were found on the property after the house was built and are now in the custody of the current owners, the Shea family.

If you visit this site, it's best to park on Beacon Road and walk around the corner and down Hobart Avenue toward Route 24. Hobart Avenue is a narrow, winding road with blind spots, so keep your eyes open.

Union

Liberty Hall
(908) 527-0400
1003 Morris Avenue (across from Kean College)

Like Boxwood Hall in Elizabeth, Liberty Hall is one of the most prominent homes in New Jersey history.

Liberty Hall was the country estate of William Livingston, the first governor of the state of New Jersey. He built the estate in 1772 on the outskirts of Elizabethtown for his retirement after a long career in law and politics in New York. He was a strident patriot: a member of the First and Second Continental Congresses and a brigadier general in command of the New Jersey militia. In 1776, after the colonies declared their independence from England, William Livingston was picked by the legislature to be the first governor of New Jersey. His son-in-law, John Jay, was, among other things, the first Chief Justice of the United States. Livingston was also a friend of Washington's, and Liberty Hall is one of the few places in New Jersey where Martha slept on her way to Washington's inauguration.

During the Revolution, Livingston was the man most respected by Americans and most hated by the other side. According to *Union County Yesterday* (see the Research chapter), Livingston survived " 'repeated attempts by the British and the Loyalists to capture him. In 1778 a reward for two thousand guineas and a pension from the crown of Great Britain during life' was offered for 'that damned rascal Governor Livingston' dead or alive. It is said that he did not sleep more than two consecutive nights in the same place; and he was seldom able to visit his beloved Liberty Hall."

Add Livingston's daughter, Sally, to the list of legendary New Jersey Revolutionary War heroines. Like Tempe Wick and Molly Pitcher, Sally Livingston displayed courage and resourcefulness under fire when a group of British officers pushed their way into the house, demanding to see her father's papers. She cooperated until the officers got close to the important material—some documents about the strength of the New Jersey militia. She then feigned embarrassment and asked that the officers go no further because the papers included correspondence between her and a gentlemen friend.

The officers, being gentlemen, complied and left the house.

William Livingston died in 1790. In 1798, the house was sold out of the family, but it was repurchased by Susan Livingston, a niece of William's, in 1811. Susan Livingston's first husband was John Kean of Beaufort, South Carolina, who died in 1796. They had a son, Peter, who inherited the house from his mother. The house remained in the Kean family until Mary Alice Barney Kean died in 1995. She willed the house to be opened to the public, and plans are under way to do just that.

Connecticut Farms Presbyterian Church
Stuyvesant Avenue near Chestnut Street
(908) 688-3164

This stone church, which sits on a small hill overlooking Route 22, was the site of a battle on June 7, 1780. The original church was burned to the ground on June 23 by British soldiers retreating from Springfield. The current structure was built two years later.

The church was the centerpiece of a small village, Connecticut Farms— so named because the first settlers were from Connecticut.

During the battle at Connecticut Farms, Hannah Caldwell, the wife of the Reverend James Caldwell, was hit by a stray bullet (see the James Caldwell Home entry in this section).

The church cemetery contains the bodies of American, Hessian, and British soldiers who died in the fighting.

There are plaques on the church and near the cemetery, and also a sign, explaining that Washington used the church as a headquarters after the first British retreat on June 7.

If you visit this site, be aware that Stuyvesant Avenue here is a very busy and fast street. There is no on-street parking in front of the church. Use the parking lot at the far end of the church.

James Caldwell Home
909 Caldwell Avenue
(908) 964-9047
HOURS: By appointment.

A few blocks west of the church is the former church parsonage. After the burning of the First Presbyterian Church in Elizabethtown (see the Elizabeth section of this chapter), the Reverend James Caldwell fled to Connecticut Farms, believing his family would be safer there.

On June 7, as fighting swirled in the area, Mrs. Caldwell was hit by a stray bullet and killed. The stories vary. Some say she was hit by accidental British fire as she worked in her kitchen and died in front of her horrified children. Some say she was purposely gunned down by a British soldier while she stood on the porch of her home (as the official Union County Seal

The Caldwell Parsonage

depicts). Others say no one can be exactly sure who fired the shot that killed her. No matter. The death of Mrs. Caldwell gave the British (and the Union County Loyalists) all the bad press they could handle. Her "murder" became a rallying cry for outraged area Patriots. If the American resolve was weakening before the invasion, as Knyphausen thought, that resolve was fortified by the death of Mrs. Caldwell.

The parsonage, too, was burned down during the British retreat. A new parsonage was built on the original foundation two years later.

The house is operated by the Union Township Historical Society and has exhibits on early life in Union. There is also an exhibit on Gen. William "Scotch Willie" Maxwell, a hero of the Connecticut Farms–Springfield fighting.

The Morris Avenue Markers
Morris Avenue

Following Morris Avenue west from Elizabeth to Union, you will see four blue-and-white or blue-and-yellow historic markers along the way.

> The first explains Liberty Hall.
>
> The second is near the intersection of Elmwood Avenue and Morris Avenue. It marks the spot where "American troops withdrew . . . west along Elmwood and Morris Avenues toward the Rahway River Bridge at the Springfield border on June 7, 1780 after heavy fighting at the First Presbyterian Church."
>
> The third is at Morris Avenue and Colonial Terrace. It explains Knyphausen's intention to "destroy Washington's army camped at Morristown" as he marched toward Springfield.
>
> The fourth is on the Union side of the Rahway River Bridge, where "American Col. Elias Dayton ordered a 4 pound four cannon to fire east on Morris Ave. at the advancing enemy. The British were driven back, and they retreated during the evening of June 7, 1780."

On the Rahway River Bridge is a plaque "to the memory of Col. Israel Angell who commanded the 2nd Rhode Island Infantry at the Battle of Springfield" on June 23, 1780.

The plaque contains this commendation from Washington: "The gallant behaviour of Col. Angell's regiment . . . at Springfield reflects the highest honour upon the officers and men. . . . They disputed an important pass with so obstinate a bravery that they lost upwards of forty killed, wounded and missing before they gave up their ground to a vast superiority of force."

Battle of Springfield Bronze Plaque

To see this plaque, park at the Washington Street Park on the Springfield side of the bridge (see the Springfield section of this chapter) and walk back across the bridge. The plaque is in the middle of the span.

Vauxhall Road Bridge Area
(near Millburn Avenue)

At the junction of Millburn Avenue and Vauxhall Road is a public parking lot that is the site of another Battle of Springfield encounter.

Having been turned back on the main road by Col. Dayton on June 7, Baron von Knyphausen split the British columns in two, sending one half down the main road and the other half to the north in hopes of surprising, and surrounding, the Americans holding down the town of Springfield.

The north column was heavily made up of American Loyalists of the Queen's Rangers. A Continental force of dragoons under Col. "Light-Horse" Harry Lee, supported by two regiments of New England troops, fought bitterly against them along the banks of a tributary of the Rahway River. The Continental troops gave ground, but slowed the attack enough to ruin Knyphausen's plan.

There is a sign on the Vauxhall Road side of the parking lot that explains the action. There is a second plaque on the concrete bridge about fifty feet up Vauxhall Road that cites the heroics of Lee, Col. Matthias Ogden, and Capt. George Walker John in discouraging the invaders. If you go to read it, keep one eye on the road . . . it's congested.

Westfield

Gallows Hill Plaque
Corner of East Broad Street and Gallows Hill Road

On November 24, 1781, an American sentry named James Morgan stopped the combative Reverend James Caldwell at Elizabethtown Point. A dispute over a package that Caldwell was carrying escalated to a point where Morgan shot and killed Caldwell.

Some said Morgan was simply acting as ordered when he detained Caldwell. But evidence surfaced at his trial that he had been paid by enemies of Caldwell to do Caldwell in. He was tried in the First Presbyterian Church (see the Presbyterian Church Cemetery entry in this section) and convicted of murdering the popular revolutionary.

Morgan was hanged on this spot, and the Westfield Bicentennial Committee has embedded a plaque in the sidewalk at the site. The plaque is right at the corner of the two streets. At first glance, it looks like a common utility plate, but a closer look yields the gallows story.

Caldwell's nine children, orphaned at his death (his wife had been shot dead at Connecticut Farms in 1780) were adopted by various prominent citizens of the time, including Elias Boudinot and the Marquis de Lafayette.

Presbyterian Church Cemetery
Corner of East Broad Street and Mountain Avenue

Across the street from the Presbyterian Church is the church cemetery, where seventy Revolutionary War soldiers are buried. A Daughters of the American Revolution plaque on a boulder was placed there in 1924. It says, "In honor of the men of Westfield buried here who fought in the war of the American Revolution that they and their descendants might enjoy the blessings of a government by the people."

According to *The WPA Guide* (see the Research chapter), the first skirmish in New Jersey where the Americans drove back the British happened on Mountain Avenue, up the street from the church: "Up Mountain Ave. in December, 1776, came in triumph a company of Jersey militia, driving 400

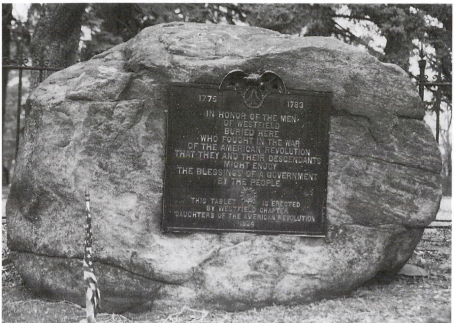

Westfield Cemetery Marked by the Daughters of the American Revolution

cattle taken from British foragers at Woodbridge. This was the first occasion in this State, as officially reported, when British troops fled from Americans."

However, there is no monument or plaque on Mountain Avenue marking the skirmish.

Sip Manor
5 Cherry Lane
(Private)

This home was originally on the corner of Newkirk Street and Bergen Avenue in Jersey City, where Cornwallis used it as a headquarters. There is a story that he ordered the hanging of three suspected spies, who swung from the willow tree behind the house the next day.

The house was moved to Westfield in 1928 as the one of the centerpieces of the Wychwood development, one of the most exclusive neighborhoods in Union County.

Upper Delaware Region

HUNTERDON, SUSSEX, AND WARREN COUNTIES

Hunterdon County's Revolutionary War activity all took place in what is now the southern part, close to present-day Mercer County. Part of the Continental army crossed into Pennsylvania at Coryell's Ferry, which today is Lambertville, during Washington's miserable retreat across New Jersey. Washington crossed the county again in 1778, this time in pursuit of the British in the days before the battle at Monmouth.

Sussex County, though it's hard to believe now, was the frontier at the time of the Revolution. Almost all the wartime bloodshed involved battles with British-backed Indians. In early 1779, Col. Joseph Brant, a Mohawk Indian with the British military commission that operated in the New Jersey–Pennsylvania–New York area for the length of war, warned the Sussex residents that they would "be treated as an enemy" if they did not pledge allegiance to the crown. Brant led a number of raids in the area, including one on Sussex Court House (now Newton).

Along the Delaware, Sussex had eight forts—no more than small homes, really—that housed small groups of soldiers to protect the residents. All but two are gone.

In the southern part of the county, the Andover Forge (now Waterloo) was a major supplier for the Continental army.

Warren County was perhaps New Jersey's quietest county during the Revolution. The sparsely populated area saw almost no action during the war. Still, there are a few things to see if you head west into the state's rural belt.

Andover (Sussex County)

Andover Mines Site
Limecrest Road

About a quarter mile before the main parking lot for Kittatinny Valley State Park is a turnoff with a small parking lot. On this state-owned land is the old Andover Mine.

Writer Mark McGarrity of *The Star-Ledger* described the area like this:

> Like some towering bicuspid waiting to be filled, the entire steep hill that from the road appears in no way unusual has been drilled out. Cored years ago, when most of the power to cut the magnetite from the rock was supplied by hand. Peering into the main pit you remember historian Vernon L. Parrington's assessment of the first one-hundred-fifty years of American history: that it was the history of work. Now Scotch pines, moss and grasses cling to the side. Bank swallows have nested wherever there is clay. And at twilight—should you chance this climb in darkness, before the chill nights set in—you can watch hordes of bats gush from the one-hundred-seventy-foot-long "haulage way," a tunnel carved through the mountain to extract the magnetite.

The Andover Mines supplied the ore for the Andover Forge, which is now at Waterloo Village (see the Waterloo Village section of this chapter).

Belvidere (Warren County)

Belvidere Cemetery
Oxford Street (next to Belvidere High School)

Buried here are a number of Revolutionary War soldiers, including Gen. William "Scotch Willie" Maxwell, a Warren County native.

Maxwell was an old soldier when the war began, having served the British during the French and Indian Wars.

During the Revolution, Maxwell was involved in the Battles of Brandywine, Germantown, Monmouth, and Springfield. He also took part in Sullivan's Expedition (see the Wallace House entry in the Somerville section, Somerset County chapter). His military record was spotty, although he had fine moments at Springfield.

He earned the name "Scotch Willie" not because of his Scotch-Irish ancestry but because he was a little too fond of Scotch whiskey.

He was elected to the New Jersey Assembly in 1783.

Hackettstown (Warren County)

Wilson House Site
176 Main Street

On this building, known locally as the "bank building" is a bronze plaque that says the home of Lt. Robert Wilson and his wife stood here. The Wilsons entertained the Washingtons—George and Martha—a number of times while the Continental army was encamped at Morristown.

The bank building is between Moore and Main Streets.

Hampton Township (Sussex County)

Unknown Soldier Monument
Cherry Lane

In the old days, this road was a main route between Pennsylvania and New York. Today it is a dead-end street off Hampton House Road, which is off Route 94/206 a couple of miles north of downtown Newton.

Part of the Continental army was marching through here in 1780 when one of the soldiers died of exhaustion. He was buried where he fell, as was customary in that day. While his identity was unknown to locals, the grave site became a minor landmark. Around the turn of the century, the Chinkchewunksa Chapter of the Daughters of the Revolution marked the grave site with a granite plaque that looks like a headstone with a small flag on top.

Hardyston Township (Sussex County)

Continental Army Encampment Site
Corner of Route 94 and Beaver Run Road

The monument here marks the encampment of Washington's army in 1779 as it marched between Newburgh, New York, and Morristown.

The monument is dedicated to Lt. John Kays. Legend has it that Washington lost a valued timepiece in this area. Kays returned to camp, found the general's watch, and was hero for a day.

Lambertville (Hunterdon County)

John Holcombe House
260 North Main Street (Route 29)
(Private)

Washington stayed here on at least two occasions, according to Susan Deckert, a D.A.R. member who has researched the general's stays in New Jersey. Deckert located Washington at this house twice: from July 28 through August 1, 1776, and on June 21–22, 1778, as his troops crossed into New Jersey from Pennsylvania in the days before the Battle of Monmouth.

At the time Washington stayed here, the house was owned by Holcombe's son Richard and his wife, Mary.

Coryell's Ferry Sites
End of Ferry Street and vicinity of Coryell Street
    and Lambert Lane

There were two spots on each side of the river for ferry landings and departures, and the boats went back and forth in a crisscross pattern. Coryell's Ferry was used four times by the Continental army, and Washington considered it a base point for his Mid-Atlantic campaigns. It was the site of three documented skirmishes. On December 9, 1776, as Washington's troops completed their retreat across New Jersey, shots were exchanged across the river near here. On February 28, 1778, the British stopped American foragers from bringing one hundred twenty-seven head of cattle into Pennsylvania. Shots were also exchanged across the river on April 4, 1778.

Continental Army Encampment Site
Bridge and North Union Streets

Part of the Continental army camped in the orchards here in June 1778, just days before the Battle of Monmouth.

Montague (Sussex County)

Battle of Conashaugh Marker
Old Mine Road

About two and one-half miles south of the intersection of Route 206 and Old Mine Road in Montague is an area off Old Mine Road that contains the Minnisink Cemetery and the Westbrook Fort.

At the Minnisink Cemetery is a monument to the thirteen American soldiers killed at the Battle of Conashaugh on April 21, 1780. The engagement is also called the Battle of Raymondskill because it took place across the Delaware near the Raymondskill Creek over in Pike County, Pennsylvania.

Nearby is an old house known as the Westbrook Fort—one of the surviving forts along the Delaware. The house today is used by the National Park Service to house rangers and their families.

Mount Airy (Hunterdon County)

Route to Battle of Monmouth
Village Road (off Old York Road) and
Mt. Airy–Harbourton Road

Between Lambertville and Ringoes is the small village of Mount Airy. A historical marker points out that the Continental army passed through in June 1778 on its way to the Battle of Monmouth.

Newton (Sussex County)

Anderson House Site
62 Main Street

Thomas Anderson was a commissary officer for the Continental army, which may have stored supplies on his property. Washington visited him on July 26, 1782, while he and his staff stayed at the Cochrane Tavern on Main and Spring Streets.

The Anderson house is now gone, but standing in its spot are the offices of Christ Episcopal Church. A historical marker on the grounds tells the story.

Sussex County Court Complex
Route 206

There were three attacks on Sussex Court House, which was in the same place as the court complex today. In one—on June 21, 1780—Lt. James Moody, a Tory spy and notorious raider, charged the jail at Sussex Court House and rescued one of his men and seven other Tories being held there. Moody's man had been captured two weeks earlier by an American major, Robert Hoops, during Moody's raid on the courthouse of June 4.

Moody, who was a farmer before the war, took up with the British when the conflict began. Known for his hit-and-run raids on the homes of prominent area Patriots, he had plans for bigger things. He once planned to kidnap Governor Livingston. He wanted to destroy the archives of Congress in Philadelphia. He planned to blow up Continental army gunpowder supplies in Morris County.

His exploits so pleased the British that after the war he went to England as the guest of Gen. Henry Clinton, the former commander in chief.

Moody's favorite hiding place was about two miles south of Newton in a wetlands area known as the Mucksaw Swamp (a map today calls this area Mucksaw Ponds). There is a rock formation nearby known as Moody's Rock or Moody's Cave, which was once a tourist attraction but is now on private property. The rock outcrop has a twenty-five-foot ledge and overhang which offered shelter to Moody and his gang. Some say that Moody's ghost haunts the area.

Oxford (Warren County)

Shippen Manor and Oxford Furnace
8 Belvidere Avenue (off Route 31)
(908) 453-4381
HOURS: First and second Sunday of every month, 1 P.M. to 4 P.M.

In the days of the Revolution, the Oxford Furnace spit out two tons of pig iron a day, which was turned into cannonballs, grapeshot, musket balls, cannons, tools, and almost any other metal product used by the Continental army. Men who worked at the furnace were paid a good wage and excused from all military obligation.

At the site today is the restored Shippen Manor, the three-story Georgian where the ironmasters lived from 1754 until 1870. In the manor are a fair number of Revolutionary War artifacts.

Across the street are the ruins of Oxford Furnace Number 1, which was built in 1741, first blasted in 1743, and last blasted 1884. The furnace was retired as the longest-running blast furnace in the country.

Ringoes (Hunterdon County)

Ringo's Tavern
1084 Old York Road
(Private)

The tavern of John Ringo on the old York Road was a busy place in colonial times. The road was the main thoroughfare between New York and Philadelphia, and Ringo's Tavern—about four miles north of Coryell's Ferry—was a natural stopping place for people who either had just crossed the river or wanted to do so first thing in the morning.

As early as 1766, Ringo's Tavern was a meeting place for the Sons of Liberty, a secret radical faction who wanted to kick England out of the colonies. It was this group that coerced all stamp agents to resign before England imposed the Stamp Act of 1766. The tavern remained a meeting place for Patriots throughout the war.

Ringo's Tavern, Ringoes

The house, which has been modernized, is marked by a historical road sign.

The Landis House
1064 Old York Road

A historical marker outside this stone house says the Marquis de Lafayette was treated there by one Dr. Gerson Craven.

Not far from here, on December 14, 1776, there was a skirmish in which a British officer was killed.

Wantage (Sussex County)

Fort Site
Route 284
(Private)

On this road, right at the border between Wantage and Unionville, New York, is one of the surviving forts of the region. There is a historical marker in front of the home.

The Landis House, Ringoes

Washington Township (Warren County)

Washington Retreat Route Marker
Asbury-Anderson Road (Route 632)

On this road near the Hunterdon County border—just south of the intersection of Port Colden–Changewater Road (Route 651) and Changewater Road (Route 645)—is a small roadside marker that says part of Washington's army passed here in late 1776 during the retreat across New Jersey.

Waterloo Village (Sussex County)

Restored Village
Waterloo Road
(973) 347-0900
HOURS: Wednesday through Sunday, 10 A.M. to 5 P.M. Mid-April
to mid-November. The village adds Tuesday to the schedule
from May until October.

This re-created village along the Musconetcong River has Lenni Lenape Indian exhibits and artifacts and a very strong nineteenth-century Morris Canal theme. But during the Revolution, the village here supported the Andover Forge, one of the most productive iron works in the nation.

The forge was started in 1760 by Joseph Turner and William Allen, the chief justice of Pennsylvania. When war broke out, these two Philadelphia Loyalists stayed loyal and supplied iron goods to the British army in America. In 1778, Congress asked the company to begin making goods for the American army, but it refused. Later the American government seized the iron works, and the four-fire, two-hammer forge began banging out Continental army war goods. A fort was built across from the valuable forge to protect it from British attack.

THE RESEARCH

Researching New Jersey's Revolutionary War history is easy. Local, county, state, and university libraries are filled with books on the war. Information about what happened and where is handily available.

It's finding out exactly where things happened that gets tricky.

As stated earlier, this book is about uncovering those historic sites that most people don't know exist. And the first thing I discovered in my library research is that there was no recent publication that lists Revolutionary War sites in New Jersey.

One of the best books (and easiest to find) is *The WPA Guide to 1930s New Jersey* (New Brunswick, N.J.: Rutgers University Press, 1986). The guide was written in 1938 by an army of writers funded by President Franklin Delano Roosevelt's Works Progress Administration. The book, part of the WPA's American Guide Series, was published by Viking Press in 1939.

Rutgers republished the book in 1986. The book has chapters on each of state's largest cities and then is divided into thirty-seven tours. In the chapters on cities, exact addresses for some historic sites are given. In the tours part, exact addresses are almost never given. The writers of *The WPA Guide* did not handcuff themselves with historical accuracy. Most times, they represent questionable stories as legend, or simply repeat stories told through generations. That's okay with me: get people interested first, let them split hairs later.

Another useful book is even older than *The WPA Guide*. In fact, that book—*Historic Roadsides in New Jersey* (Philadelphia: Society of Colonial Wars in New

Jersey, 1928)—lists more sites than any other, but again, without exact addresses.

Two other useful books I found were about twenty-five years old, published in time to capitalize on the Bicentennial fervor of 1976.

The Bicentennial Guide to the American Revolution (New York: Saturday Review Press/E. P. Dutton, 1974) was written by Sol Stember and published in three volumes—one on New England, one on the middle colonies, and one on the south. The New Jersey section of the middle colonies book lists twenty-three sites—all the places you'd expect, such as Fort Lee, Trenton, Princeton, Monmouth, Morristown. The book does not wander too far from the beaten path and it uncovers no surprise sites. Anyone fairly familiar with New Jersey Revolutionary war sites will recognize every place listed in Stember's book.

But for tourists, the book is an excellent resource because what Stember does best is give directions. The book is organized by event—such as the Battle of Trenton—and Stember not only takes you through the action, visiting the existing landmarks along the way, he tells you how to get there. The author lists exact addresses of sites, using twentieth-century highway and road designations to get you to your eighteenth-century destination.

The other book from this time period is *Landmarks of the American Revolution* (Harrisburg, Pa.: Stackpole Books, 1973) by Col. Mark M. Boatner III. The West Point–educated colonel lists thirty-nine New Jersey sites, and goes farther afield than Stember, including sites along the Mullica River and deep in South Jersey. *Landmarks* is arranged alphabetically, so chronological history is left disjointed. The book is also a little uneven in that sometimes the colonel goes off on long-winded strategic tangents about minor sites, while short-shrifting others. His Battle of Springfield description fills four pages, for instance, while he devotes four paragraphs to Morristown National Historical Park. He does, however, uncover a couple of gems—the Pulaski Monument outside of Tuckerton, for instance—which makes the book interesting reading.

Also uneven are the colonel's directions. Boatner writes that the Pulaski Monument (see the Shore Counties chapter) is located "at a bend in Radio Rd., somewhat less than three miles from the center of Tuckerton."

The monument is actually in Little Egg Harbor Township, at least six miles from Tuckerton center. It is off a little side street that intersects with Radio Road, called Kosciusko Road. (Kosciusko, of course, was Lithuanian-born Thaddeus Kosciusko—sometimes spelled Kosciuszko—a French-trained military engineer who helped the American cause in the defense of the Delaware River and in New York State.) Sure enough, a block down Kosciusko Road is a street called South Pulaski Street (there is no North, East, West, or just plain Pulaski Street). At the intersection of the two streets is the monument, which documents what is known as the Little Egg Harbor Massacre.

Historic Roadsides in New Jersey is organized by county and lists about two hundred colonial sites—only about half of which have true Revolutionary War significance. *Historic Roadsides,* being a society book, also lists a fair number of irrelevant sites—except that someone in the society was probably a descendant of the owner of the historic site.

Unfortunately, the book lists all sites—even the most important—with little or no historic detail. Here is the book's entire entry on the Wallace House in Somerville: "Washington's Headquarters for six months during the winter and spring 1778–79, now owned by the Revolutionary Memorial Society of New Jersey and used as a museum."

A perhaps bigger problem is that *Historic Roadsides* fails to give a traveler any instruction on how to find any of these the sites, except to say what town they're in. You could forgive the septuagenarian guide for this except that the book bills itself as travel companion for motorists. The preface states:

"In this day when distance is made unimportant by the motor vehicle, and we can in a day cover a mileage which would have taken many days in Colonial times, there is no excuse for unfamiliarity or lack of knowledge of the historic spots in one's own state."

Can't you see all those amateur historians overheating their Model Ts as they putter around aimlessly, trying to find the sites in *Historic Roadsides?*

Despite the lack of directions, I had great success using *Historic Roadsides* because most of the sites listed in the book are in the downtown areas of New Jersey towns. Since towns were smaller in 1928—and even smaller in 1778—many of the historic sites are easy to find once you discover the old part of town.

Many of the sites listed in *Historic Roadsides* still exist and while the book is chintzy with the facts, it does one important thing: it lists many sites marked by organizations like the Sons of the American Revolution and the Daughters of the American Revolution. These organizations in the early part of the century went on a campaign to memorialize birthplaces and homes of Revolutionary War figures, and places where something significant happened. For instance, an S.A.R. plaque at the base of the flagpole monument at

Washington Rock in Green Brook (see the Somerset County chapter) reads in part: "From this rock General George Washington watched the movements of British forces during the anxious months of May and June 1777. . . . Lest we forget."

The D.A.R. was especially adept at marking cemeteries where Revolutionary War soldiers are buried, whether or not they were killed in battle.

In trying to track down the exact addresses of monument sites in *Historic Roadsides,* I contacted a number of historical organizations in an effort to procure their lists. Anglo-American pedigree groups of this type are struggling to survive. The member numbers are shrinking and the remaining members are growing old. It's too bad. These groups have been caretakers of mainstream American history for a long time. Without their work in documenting our past with plaques and memorials, so much of our history would be plowed under.

Unfortunately, it appears their work is done. The New Jersey Society of the Sons of the American Revolution lists fifty-nine monuments and memorials. The first batch was dedicated in the 1890s, the last in 1961. There have been almost forty years without a new dedication.

I found the S.A.R. monument list by visiting the Abraham Clark House in Roselle (see the Union County chapter). Inside is a small museum with a number of Revolutionary War artifacts. I list a number of other historical society houses and libraries in the body of this book that hold public hours. (As for joining, while one can't change his or her lineage to gain entry into a hereditary society like the D.A.R. or S.A.R., there are plenty of other community and county historical groups that always need members.)

The list I got from the Abraham Clark chapter in Roselle gave no exact addresses, although it yielded some strong hints. Here's a typical entry:

"1913, Oct. 4—Monument to Richard Stockton, signer of the Declaration of Independence, in Stony Brook Friends burying ground, Princeton, New Jersey."

The 1998 translation is simple, with a little investigation. Stockton is buried at the Princeton Friends–Quaker Meeting House, at the junction of Mercer and Quaker Roads, just south of the Princeton Battlefield (see the Mercer County chapter).

The monument lists opened my eyes to a whole other world of site documentation. Now, I wanted to know more. I was especially interested in finding a catalog of all the places marked by those blue-and-cream signs you see posted next to historic homes and other sites on New Jersey roadsides. I knew that somewhere in the maze of Trenton's state offices, someone would have a list of all historical markers and monuments. The next step in my discovery process was to contact the state and find out who had that list.

This was easier said than done.

I called a half dozen state offices that sounded like they should have the list. Each time, I was referred to another office or division. Soon, I saw a pattern. Each time I called a new place, they referred me back to the people who had referred me to them. After a week of go-rounds, I realized no such list existed.

One person who did help was Terry Karschner from the state's Historic Preservation office. Karschner knew of a Revolutionary War site survey that was done in 1970 by the New Jersey Department of Environmental Protection's Parks and Forestry division. The survey was supposed to be completed by the Bicentennial, but it was left unfinished because of insufficient funding. Karschner dug out the survey for me and made some notations about the historical significance of many of the places.

The sites in the survey range from the well known to the obscure. Unfortunately, while the well-known sites are listed with accompanying addresses, the obscure remain, well, obscure. Take for instance two listings on the same page in the Morris County section. The first reads: "Sayre House (where Mad Anthony Wayne stayed during Morristown encampment), 31 Ridgedale Ave., Madison."

And then, "Site of French Army Encounter, Hanover Township."

No clues there. As of this writing, I still have no idea where this site is.

Armed with this survey, the monument list and the three books (and the knowledge that all New Jersey county libraries have extensive local history collections), I hit the road and set out to discover New Jersey's Revolutionary trail.

One of my first trips was to the Monmouth Battlefield State Park in Freehold and Manalapan Townships. (See the Shore Counties chapter.)

There, hanging in the visitors' center, is a 28-by-48-inch map called *Battles and Skirmishes of the American Revolution.*

The map is an extraordinary piece of New Jersey history documentation. It lists an incredible 787 sites, including encounters between British and American forces, and dustups between American revolutionaries and Americans who stayed loyal to the king. It also lists a number of sea battles off the Jersey coast and in the Delaware Bay.

When I first saw the *Battles and Skirmishes* map, I was amazed at the number of entries on it. As with many New Jerseyans, my former knowledge of New Jersey battles stopped at the majors: Trenton, Princeton, Monmouth, Springfield, and a few others.

This map was a black-and-white illustration of how much activity there was here—and how much I had to learn.

The first edition of the map was done in 1945 by John D. Alden, the historian for the New Jersey Society of the Sons of the American Revolution. The map was updated in 1965 by S.A.R. member D. Stanton Hammond. Hammond wanted the map reproduced for the nation's Bicentennial celebration and brought it to the state. It fell under the auspices of the Bureau of Geology and Topography and the Bureau of Archives and History.

(Today, you can get the map for a mere five dollars by writing the Department of Environmental Protection Maps and Publications office at 428 East State Street, Trenton, 08625, or calling [609] 777-1038 or 1039.)

The map is as true to colonial New Jersey as possible. Old road systems are marked. Cape May is extended to reflect what it looked like in "the decade of 1770–1780," that is, with two hundred fewer years of erosion. Sandy Hook, on the other hand was smaller. But more important, the map lists all the battles and skirmish sites by their colonial names . . . Spanktown (Rahway) . . . Quibbletown (Piscataway) . . . Decker's Fort (Wantage) . . . Bacon's Neck (Greenwich) . . . English Neighborhood (Cliffside Park, Englewood, Englewood Cliffs, Fort Lee, and Leonia area).

Major battles—Trenton, Princeton, Monmouth—are listed in red, highlighted by crossed swords. Smaller battles and incidents—such as Hancock's Bridge, the Baylor Massacre, Chestnut Neck—are also marked in red, with smaller crossed swords.

The rest of the sites are listed in black.

The information on the battles, skirmishes, and incidents is confined to general place and date. There are no exact addresses and almost no details: Here is a typical entry:

SAMPTOWN

MAR 9-77

JUN 26-77

Every now and then, the map provides a hint of detail, especially for events like winter encampments or other nonbattle circumstances. The Greenwich entry, for instance, says "Tea Destroyed." Some of the naval encounters, too, come with a little description.

JULY-78

14 BRITISH TRANSPORTS TAKEN OFF EGG HARBOR, BOUND
    PHILADELPHIA TO NEW YORK

And,

VESSELS OUTBOUND FROM DELAWARE TAKEN BY BRITISH CRUISERS

OCT 13-79	BRIG SALLY
DEC 4-79	LADY WASHINGTON
DEC 4-79	BRIG THREE SISTERS
JAN 17-81	SEVERAL VESSELS

Soon after seeing the map, I went to Trenton to pick up a copy of my own.

I was discouraged that the map listed no exact locations, but I thought it would be useful for investigative purposes. In Trenton, I learned that the map had an accompanying booklet: *Battles and Skirmishes in New Jersey of the American Revolution,* by David C. Munn (Trenton, N.J.: New Jersey Department of Environmental Protection, 1976). But the booklet has long been out of print and is no longer available through the state.

Within weeks, however, I found three copies of the booklet. One was at the Thomas Clarke House (the visitors' center and museum) at Princeton Battlefield State Park. One was back at the Abraham Clark House in Roselle. The other was in the Rutgers University library. I borrowed the copy from the Abraham Clark House and now have a copy of my own.

The booklet's preface spells out its limitations:

The intention of the map is to suggest the approximate sites of the various battles and skirmishes that occurred during the Revolutionary War rather than pinpoint the exact locations. Along the same lines, this pamphlet will provide only brief descriptions of the actions. . . .

The actual number of violent events that occurred in New Jersey during the Revolutionary War years can never be determined. The era in New Jersey begins with the "tea party" at Greenwich on December 22, 1774, and ends with a naval encounter on March 3, 1783, nearly nine years later.

The lack of primary source materials makes local actions, both British and American, extremely difficult to discover and document. . . .

We have tried to include on the map every overt or hostile action by either side that could be documented. . . . there are many examples of hostile actions that did not involve shots but they are significant to the course of the war and are included. In many instances events may be nothing more than opposing sides shouting obscenities at each other from safe distances.

Despite the lack of exact locations, the *Battles and Skirmishes* booklet is good reading. The brief descriptions are action-packed:

Bound Brook, January 6, 1777
> British light horse raid Bound Brook and a Tory named Stewart shoots Benjamin Boloney as he hides in his cellar.

And are filled with surprising detail:

English Neighborhood, June 4, 1779
> Small party of Col. Abraham (Van) Buskirk's men surprise party of rebels, takes two prisoners, William Wirts and Henry Bastion, "both noted spys and robbers."

The booklet also reiterates the point that the Revolution was truly a civil war. It identifies a number of hot spots like English Neighborhood (Englewood), where all the conflict is between local rebels and local Tories.

One of those hot spots was Hopperstown, the present-day Ho-ho-kus, where there were five skirmishes between late 1776 and early 1780. Here, you can see how fighting escalates in an area:

Hopperstown, December 27, 1776
> British and Tory force take Garrett Hopper and six or seven other Whig farmers prisoners.

Hopperstown, April 26, 1777
> Party of new levies carry off Capt. Wynant Van Zandt and three others from Garrett Hopper's neighborhood.

Hopperstown, April 21, 1779
> British kill Capt. Jonathan Hopper during raid.

Hopperstown, March 23, 1780
> Two detachments from New York penetrate neutral ground and attack rear of rebel cantonments at Hopperstown. Several prisoners taken, but major action is avoided by Americans.

Hopperstown, April 16, 1780
> Americans lose one major, two captains, four lieutenants and about 40 rank and file during raid by British.

The booklet—like this book—relies on secondary sources. In addition, it lists the source for each entry. Most of the information comes from the New Jersey State Archives. The battles and skirmishes are listed in alphabetical order by place, and Munn acknowledges that such organization "detracts from the general overview of the war in that it presents events out of sequence."

To get a better overview, he recommends a booklet called *New Jersey in the American Revolution, 1763–1783: A Chronology,* by Dennis P. Ryan (Trenton, N.J.: New Jersey Historical Commission, 1974). And so do I.

Ryan's booklet is sold in most state-run war-site parks. I bought mine at the Old Barracks Museum in Trenton. The book gives scant detail on violent engagements and no exact site locations, but it does a good job tracking the prewar and wartime political and legislative machinations of the New Jersey governing bodies:

> April 18, 1778—County commissioners are to seize the personal property of Loyalists found guilty by a jury of twenty-four freeholders. The property will be sold or leased to tenants who pay rent to the commissioners.
>
> June 20, 1778—A legislative act encourages the manufacture of paper by granting militia exemptions to workers.
>
> June 20, 1778—The export of provisions such as wheat, beef, and livestock is prohibited under penalty of seizure.

You can see from these entries that the Jersey lawmakers had one eye on the economy and one eye on the war effort.

The book also adds some nice domestic touches:

> April 1, 1778—Congregations from Essex, Morris, Middlesex, and Somerset Counties send clothing to sick and injured soldiers.

And, of course, there are the blow-by-blow accounts of fighting.

> May 7, 1778—A British raid in Bordentown results in the destruction of the unfinished American frigates *Washington* and *Effingham.* British units burn a number of houses in the town before returning to their ships.

Other great sources of information are the brochures, pamphlets, and booklets you can find at historic sites or county historical societies. But to collect them, you have to get out on the road and see something.

OTHER WORKS CONSULTED

Anderson, John R. *Shepard Kollock: Editor for Freedom.* Chatham Historical Society, 1975.

Boatner, Mark III. *Encyclopedia of the American Revolution.* New York: David McKay, 1974.

Cavanaugh, Cam. *In Lights and Shadows: Morristown in Three Centuries.* The Joint Free Public Library of Morristown and Morris Township.

Durnin, Richard G. *George Washington in Middlesex County, New Jersey.* North Brunswick, N.J.: Middlesex County Cultural and Heritage Commission, 1989.

Dwyer, William M. *The Day Is Ours! An Inside View of the Battles of Trenton and Princeton.* 1988; reprint, New Brunswick, N.J.: Rutgers University Press, 1998.

Leiby, Adrian C. *The Revolutionary War in the Hackensack Valley.* New Brunswick, N.J.: Rutgers University Press, 1962.

McMahon, William. *South Jersey Towns: History and Legend.* New Brunswick, N.J.: Rutgers University Press, 1973.

The Pictorial Guide to the Historic Buildings of Bridgeton. This document is available at the Cumberland County tourism office.

Union County Yesterday. Published by the Union County Cultural and Heritage Advisory Board in 1981.

INDEX

Page numbers in boldface refer to main references for Revolutionary War sites.
Page numbers in italics refer to photographs.

ABOUT THE AUTHOR

MARK DI IONNO, an award-winning journalist, is the assistant managing editor, Local News, at *The Star-Ledger*, the largest circulation newspaper in New Jersey. His first book, *New Jersey's Coastal Heritage: A Guide* (Rutgers University Press, 1996), won the New Jersey Studies Academic Alliance Award. Born and raised in New Jersey, Di Ionno now lives in Mountain Lakes. He is the father of six children, some of whom "kid-tested" the attractions in this book.